Vedic Machine

Dev Bhattacharyya

CONTENTS

DEDICATION

To the Lord

He who knows the Lord within
For him church-doors are always open.

*

Mithoo, Dea, Sonne, Kamryn, Sha
Arsha Vidya Gurukulam
Createspace and Amazon

Special thanks to Debol Gupta and Shri Gupta
This venture would have never been complete without them

PREFACE

With the coming of age and maturity in Internet of things IoT, Do it yourself DIY kits, Analog and electronic sensors, it set me back on the memory lane to where I started several decades ago tinkering with these gadgets. It surged an interest with Vedic translations I was busy with and quickly did I amass a lot of these tiny MCU - micro controller units that serve the purpose of this book.

While Moore's law is now a thing of the past, the coming of open source software and hardware have paved the way for collaborative professionalism. It is perhaps not too early to say that the professional is back - the one who can write software that defines business. Maybe I was abrupt in passing a judgement, perhaps you knew it was coming - yes, software and knowledge workers are defining new industries. That there is an intimate connection of technology to the divine, there is no doubt; though it is evident there is a greater association to the worldly material.

This book is about bringing the Vedic art of the ancient into the technology era of open source hardware and software to qualify the merit of what Vedic knowledge was. A neo-Vedic twist to the old art, practice and culture. The Vedas defined the initiator and the terminator. Vedanta brought about dharma (duties), karma (fate) and nyaya (justice); Tantra taught us grace and surrender or bhakti. This book is a return to the roots - the Vedic message and the appropriateness and attractiveness of its outcome, of physical and logical separations.

VEDIC MACHINES

Vedic definition of wealth is abundance of spiritual knowledge and health that enables its enjoyment. The ancient enjoyed direct connection with the deities from this powerful knowledge. What was routine in the yesteryears is but an enigma today.

There was no concept of rise in profession or promotions or even acquisition of vehicles; only the noble and monarchy enjoyed such privileges. These concepts are but recent additions to ancient texts. The *Panchanga* (the Vedic Almanac / Calendar) spoke of quality of time appropriate for commune with the deities and the supreme, the hour to supplicate health and remedies. It set a discipline to lifestyle as a proactive method than the reactive system of medicine that has evolved today.

Cardiac monitoring systems, heart rate machines, pulse monitoring systems are systems of modern times. The ancient relied on *Ayurveda* and pulse checks through touch. The sensitivity of the touch could reveal the 'doshas', especially the primary 'dosha'. Some of these techniques can be viewed as patterns through sensory devices that can mimic the sensitivity and bring the ancient practice to science and technology. The primary center for Nadi Shastra on which some of the book is based on is

Vaitheeswarankoil, near Chidambaram in Tamil Nadu, a state in Southern India. Lord Shiva incarnated as a vaidhya - a doctor to ease the miseries of his devotees. Until the late 1930's, Nadi remained shrouded in cult and mystery, not practiced by Astrologers then.

We present here undistorted Vedic practices through different devices, software, enclosures, peripheral attachments that may be both a fun thing and an in-depth analysis of ancient practices.

The devices or software described in this book do not replace professional medical practice, medical equipment as used in clinics. These devices are indicative only and applicable in monitoring healthy lifestyles and supplement medical advice. If in doubt, the reader is advised to ask a doctor, physician or a medical practitioner on the usage of these devices.

An electrocardiogram (ECG) measures electrical activity on the body surface generated by the heart. ECG measurement information is collected by electrodes placed at select locations on the body. The signal is characterized by six peaks and valleys labeled P, Q, R, S, T, and U.

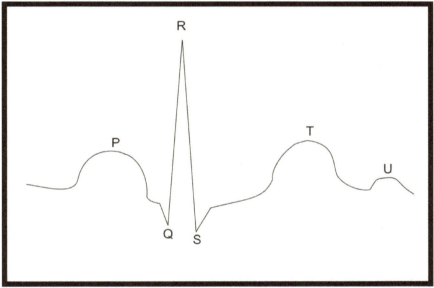

Figure 1 - ECG Graph Plotted

An overview of a typical analog ECG topology is illustrated. An electronic circuit is proposed which performs analog-to-digital conversion, digital filtering, and digital amplification by using a Microcontroller, an integrated "system on a chip" that combines an Analog Digital converter, microcontroller and flash memory. The article discusses considerations in the choice of components and programming of the Microcontroller.

Front end of the proposed Vedic heart machine deals with extremely weak signals ranging from 0.5 mV to 5.0 mV, combined with up to ±300 mV, resulting from the electrode-skin contact, plus a common-mode component of up to 1.5 V, resulting from the potential between the electrodes and ground. The useful bandwidth of an ECG signal, depending on the application, can range from 0.5 Hz to 50 Hz for monitoring applications in intensive care units; up to 1 kHz for late-potential measurements like pacemaker detection. A standard clinical ECG application has a bandwidth of 0.05 Hz to 100 Hz.

ECG signals may become distorted with noise from power-line interference, variable contact between the electrode and the skin, impedance changes caused by changes in the electrode-skin contact, muscular contraction, respiration, electromagnetic interference from other electronic devices, noise coupled from other high frequency electronic devices. For meaningful and accurate detection, it is best to filter out or discard all these noise sources.

The illustration below shows a block diagram of a typical single-channel electrocardiograph. All filtering happens in the analog domain, while the microcontroller is used for communication and other downstream activities.

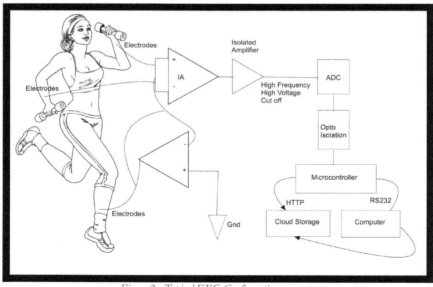

Figure 2 - Typical EKG Configuration

An electrocardiogram test checks for problems with the electrical activity of your heart. EKG translates the heart's electrical activity into graphs. Spikes and dips in the graphs are the "waves". The heart is a muscular pump with four chambers. Two upper chambers are "atria", and two lower chambers are "ventricles". A natural electrical system causes the heart muscle to contract and pump blood through the heart to the lungs and the rest of the body.

EKG results may look normal even when a heart disease is present. The EKG should always be interpreted along with other telltale symptoms, past health, physical examination, and other test results. An electrocardiogram cannot predict whether you will have a heart attack. This is where the Vedic Principles come in.

At first, an EKG test done during a heart attack may look normal or unchanged from a previous EKG. So the EKG may be repeated over several hours and days called serial EKGs to look for changes. Sometimes EKG abnormalities can be detected only during exercise or while symptoms are present. To check for these changes in the heartbeat, an ambulatory EKG or stress EKG may be performed.

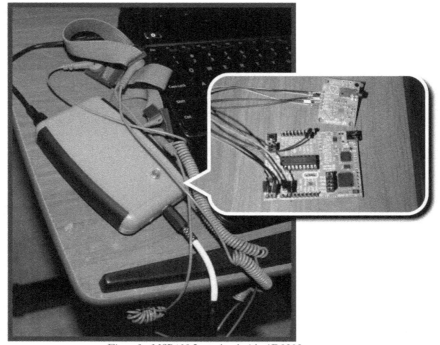

Figure 3 - MSP430 Launchpad with AD8232

Combined device is a low cost micro controller based system using Texas Instruments MSP 430 G2553, Basic Heart Rate Monitor (from Sparkfun) based on AD8232. Three lead cardiac cable for chest or arms and legs, Vedic Cardio Software available as download and explained in this book and a cable to connect to laptop USB. Software can run on Windows XP, Vista, 7 and 8 (both 32 and 64 bit operating systems), Linux (32 and 64 bit), Mac OSX.

MSP430 with AD8232 is a simple device, based on rather modest architecture principles. It is an appropriate time to understand the workings of a microcontroller unit. The UART section as shown in figure 3 allows the MCU to communicate with a host computer, the I2C works with other MCUs and similar devices. The SPI is a good place to connect segment displays, Bluetooth, SD Cards and others. Digital connectors are great for photodiodes, LEDs, Pulldown resistors. For the EKG/ECG devices, we will use the Analog inputs to collect information from an ADC (Analog to Digital) sensor.

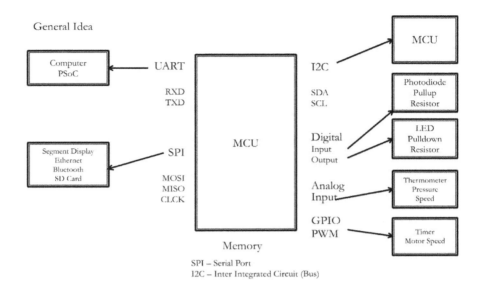

General Idea

Figure 4 - General Idea of How the MCU is organized

❋

While all connection abilities unlock interesting questions on what can be connected and how many, the thing to remember is that the devices need to be kept simple to ensure security and efficiency.

```
/*
 * msp430_ad8232_ekg.ino
 *
 *   Copyright and Product Acknowledgments:
 *      TI EXP430G2553 Launchpad
 *      Sparkfun AD8232 EKG Single channel sensor
 *   Distributed under Open Source Apache License
 *   Please do not remove the copyright notice
 */

// Sparkfun AD8232 connected to
// MSP430 G2553 Launchpad
// *********************************
// 3.3V * *                  * * Gnd
//      * * A0/Output        * *
//      * *                  * *
//      * *                  * *
//      * *                  * *
//      * *                  * *
//      * *                  * *
//      * *                  * * Lo+/13
```

7

```
//         * *                    * * Lo-/12
//         * *                    * *
// *********************************
```

```
#include "energia.h"
int starttime;
int activetime;
int previoustime = 0;
int cnt = 0;
volatile unsigned int inADC = 0;
#define PLPLUS P2_5
#define PLMINUS P2_4

void setup() {
  // initialize the serial communication:
  Serial.begin(9600);
  pinMode(PLPLUS, INPUT);//Setup for leads detecting LO +
  pinMode(PLMINUS, INPUT);//Setup for leads detecting LO -
  starttime = millis();
}

void loop() {

  if ((digitalRead(PLPLUS) == 1) ||
      (digitalRead(PLMINUS) == 1)) {
    // Leads not connected
    Serial.println('!');
  } else{
    // send the value of analog input 0:
    inADC = analogRead(A0);   // PIN_06
    Serial.print("ADC,");
    Serial.print(inADC);
    Serial.print(",");
    Serial.println(activetime);
    ++cnt;
  }
  //Wait for a bit to keep serial data from saturating
  delay(1);
  activetime = millis() - starttime;
}
```

Listing - msp430_ad8232_ekg.ino

AD8232 development board is approximately the size of a quarter and has five to six connections. In the code snippet above the LO+ and LO- are connected to MSP430 Launchpad pins 13 and 12. The Output from the AD8232 is connected to the Analog Input pin A0 just below the 3.3 V supply. The AD8232 can be joined to a five-volt supply as in case of ATMEL processors in Arduino, but at five volts, it picks more noise than in 3.3 V.

Basic Heart Monitor

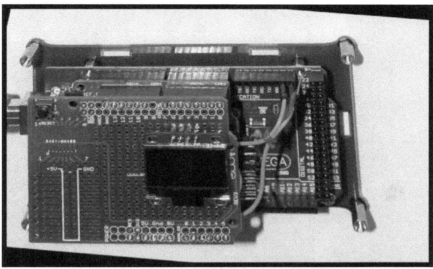

Figure 5 - Mega with Olimex ECG/EKG Shield and OLED

Extending the Simple Heart machine to a three lead system with a different Microcontroller, an EKG/EMG frontend from Olimex that has the potential to be clustered to monitor six channels. The examples in this book are shown for single channel. With a jumper setting and adding five other such boards, the device can be extended to a larger configuration.

For the device, I designed a shield (a booster pack) that can be mounted on a typical Arduino Mega hardware to house the small 1.8-inch LCD screen and Olimex EKG/EMG board. Olimex Ltd is a leading provider for development tools and programmers for embedded market. Besides, with the help of Acrylic boards, forty-centimeter spacers and M3 screws, you can construct a professional grade cardio equipment that will double up as a Vedic almanac.

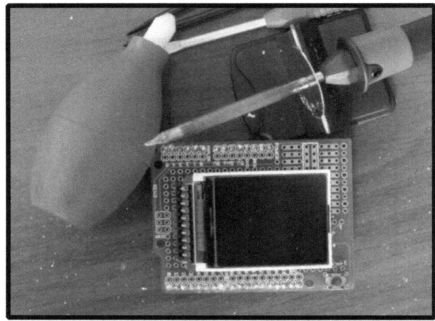

Figure 6- The Making of a SSD7735 TFT Shield

The code snippet below shows the Arduino with Olimex ECG/EMG sensors at work.

```
/*
 * sketch: mega_olimex_st7735_agniheart.ino
 *  Copyright and Product Acknowledgments:
 *      Arduino Mega: Arduico.cc
 *      Olimex EKG/EMG Hardware / Software:
 *      https://www.olimex.com/Products/Duino/Shields
 *      /SHIELD-EKG-EMG/
 *      LCD Driver: Adafruit
 *      https://github.com/adafruit/Adafruit_SSD1306
 *      Arduino Board: SainSmart Mega 2560
 *      LCD Screen: DiyMall 0.96" OLED SSD3306 Screen
 *      White Display
 *      Shield: GikFun Prototype Shield for Arduino
 */
#include <compat/deprecated.h>
#include <FlexiTimer2.h>
#include <SPI.h>
#include <Wire.h>
#include <Adafruit_GFX.h>
#include <Adafruit_ST7735.h>
#include "Panchanga.h"
```

```
#define SAMPFREQ 256
// ADC sampling rate 256
#define TIMER2VAL (1024/(SAMPFREQ))
// Set 256Hz sampling frequency
volatile unsigned char CurrentCh = 0;
//Current channel being sampled.
volatile unsigned int ADC_Value = 0;
//ADC current value
#define TFT_CS     10
#define TFT_RST    0
#define TFT_DC     8
#define TFT_SCLK 52
#define TFT_MOSI 50
Adafruit_ST7735 display = Adafruit_ST7735(TFT_CS, TFT_DC,
TFT_MOSI, TFT_SCLK, TFT_RST);

// Needed by Panchanga
uint8_t nDay = 6;
uint8_t nDD = 11;
uint8_t nMM = 4;
unsigned int nYY = 2015;
uint8_t nHour = 23;
uint8_t nMin = 18;
int nTZ = -4;
char buf[2];
char sbuf[15];
Panchanga pch;

void setup() {
  // Set the heart machine first
  noInterrupts();  // Disable all interrupts
    // before initialization

  FlexiTimer2::set(TIMER2VAL, Timer2_Overflow_ISR);
  FlexiTimer2::start();

  // Serial Port
  Serial.begin(57600);

  // Enable all interrupts after initialization
  // has been completed
  interrupts();
  // Heart machine done

  doPanchanga();
}

void doPanchanga() {
  // Do the Panchanga Next
  pch.initialize_panchanga(nDD, nMM, nYY, nHour,
    nMin, nTZ);
```

```
    delay(200);

    display.initR(INITR_BLACKTAB);
       // initialize a ST7735S chip, black tab
    display.fillScreen(ST7735_BLACK);

    drawtext("Heart Machine", ST7735_WHITE, 20, 10);
    drawtext("Panchanga");
    display.setTextSize(0);
    sprintf(buf, "%d", pch.n_tithi);
    display.setCursor(0, 18);
    display.println("Tithi:");
    display.println(buf);
    display.display();
    delay(2000);
}

void drawtext(char *text, uint16_t color, uint8_t x,
uint8_t y) {
    display.setCursor(x, y);
    display.setTextColor(color);
    display.setTextWrap(true);
    display.print(text);
}

void Timer2_Overflow_ISR() {
    ADC_Value = analogRead(CurrentCh);
    // Spit out the values
    Serial.print("ADC, ");
    Serial.println(ADC_Value);
}

void loop() {
    __asm__ __volatile__ ("sleep");
}
```

Listing - mega_olimex_st7735_agniheart.ino

Notice the code refers to the Panchanga or Vedic Almanac system. The Adafruit version of SSD 7735 comes as an Arduino Shield. Which means it can be mounted on the Arduino Mega 2560 MCU board. The recommended connections from Adafruit are to connect pins 10 and 8 to the TFT CS and DC. Alternatively, you can buy the SSD 7735 LCD from the OEM market and mount it yourself on a Shield. I used an OLED with similar configuration. The Arduino goes on the bottom, the Olimex ECG/EMG Shield mounted on it and finally the LCD or OLED display on top.

The Code Snippet below uses the SSD3306 OLED.

```
/*
 * sketch: mega_olimex_agniheart.ino
 *
 *   Created on: Apr 24, 2015
 *       Author: DevbNJ
 *   Copyright and Product Acknowledgments:
 *       Arduino Mega: Arduico.cc
 *       Olimex EKG/EMG Hardware / Software:
 *
https://www.olimex.com/Products/Duino/Shields/SHIELD-EKG-
EMG/
 *       LCD Driver: Adafruit
 *       https://github.com/adafruit/Adafruit_SSD1306
 *       Arduino Board: SainSmart Mega 2560
 *       LCD Screen: DiyMall 0.96" OLED SSD3306 Screen
 *       White Display
 *       Shield: GikFun Prototype Shield for Arduino
 */
#include <compat/deprecated.h>
#include <FlexiTimer2.h>
#include <SPI.h>
#include <Wire.h>
#include <Adafruit_GFX.h>
#include <Adafruit_SSD1306.h>
#include "Panchanga.h"

#define SAMPFREQ 256                        // ADC sampling
rate 256
#define TIMER2VAL (1024/(SAMPFREQ))         // Set 256Hz
sampling frequency
volatile unsigned char CurrentCh = 0;       //Current channel
being sampled.
volatile unsigned int ADC_Value = 0;        //ADC current
value
#define OLED_RESET 4
Adafruit_SSD1306 display(OLED_RESET);
#define LOGO16_GLCD_HEIGHT 16
#define LOGO16_GLCD_WIDTH  16

#if (SSD1306_LCDHEIGHT != 64)
#error("Height incorrect, please fix Adafruit_SSD1306.h!");
#endif

// Needed by Panchanga
uint8_t nDay = 6;
uint8_t nDD = 11;
uint8_t nMM = 4;
unsigned int nYY = 2015;
uint8_t nHour = 23;
uint8_t nMin = 18;
int nTZ = -4;
char buf[2];
```

```
char sbuf[15];
Panchanga pch;

void setup() {
  // Set the heart machine first
  noInterrupts();   // Disable all interrupts before
initialization

  FlexiTimer2::set(TIMER2VAL, Timer2_Overflow_ISR);
  FlexiTimer2::start();

  // Serial Port
  Serial.begin(57600);

  // Enable all interrupts after initialization has been
completed
  interrupts();
  // Heart machine done

  doPanchanga();
}

void doPanchanga() {
  // Do the Panchanga Next
  pch.initialize_panchanga
    (nDD, nMM, nYY, nHour, nMin, nTZ);

  delay(200);

  // Set the OLED Now
  display.begin(SSD1306_SWITCHCAPVCC, 0x3C);
  // Clear the buffer.
  display.clearDisplay();
  display.setTextSize(2);
  display.setTextColor(WHITE);

  display.setCursor(0, 0);
  display.println("CardioAgni");
  display.setTextSize(0);
  display.setCursor(0, 18);
  display.println("EKG/EMG with");
  display.setCursor(0, 28);
  display.println("Passive Electrodes");
  display.setCursor(0, 38);
  display.println("Vedic Machine");
  display.display();

  delay(10000);

  display.clearDisplay();
  display.setTextSize(2);
  display.setTextColor(WHITE);
```

```
display.setCursor(0, 0);
display.println("Panchanga");
display.setTextSize(0);
sprintf(buf, "%d", pch.n_tithi);
display.setCursor(0, 18);
display.println("Tithi:");
display.println(buf);
display.display();
delay(2000);
}

void Timer2_Overflow_ISR() {
  ADC_Value = analogRead(CurrentCh);
  // Spit out the values
  Serial.print("ADC, ");
  Serial.println(ADC_Value);
}

void loop() {
  __asm__ __volatile__ ("sleep");
}
```

    Listing - mega_olimex_agniheart.ino

Let me now introduce you to the Panchanga Code running on the microcontroller.

```
/*
 * Panchanga.h
 *
 *  Created on: Apr 11, 2015
 *      Author: DevbNJ
 */

#ifndef JOTIZ_PANCHANGA_H_
#define JOTIZ_PANCHANGA_H_

class Panchanga {
  public:
    const double pi = 3.14159265359;
    const double d2r = 3.14159265359 / 180;
    const double r2d = 180 / 3.14159265359;
    char wd[];
    double lMoon, lMoon1, lSun, skar, lMoonYoga, lSunYoga;
    double ayanamsa;
    int n_wday, n_tithi, n_naksh, n_karana, n_yoga,
    panch, transitDate;
    char s_wday, s_tithi, s_naksh, s_karana, s_yoga;
    unsigned int kyear, kmonth, kday, khour,
    kminute, ksecond;

    double computeMoon( double jd );
```

15

```
    double computeSun(double jd);
    void initialize_panchanga(uint8_t dd, uint8_t mm, int
yy, uint8_t hi, uint8_t mi, int tz);

  private:
    double fix360(double v);
    double nutation( double jd );
    double computeAyanamsa( double jd );
    double kepler(double m, double xe, double re);
    double mdy2julian(long m, long d, long y);
    double dTime (double jd);
    void calData(double jd);
    unsigned int tithi (double jd, long n1, double tzone,
int len);
    double novolun (double jd, long knv);
};

#endif /* JOTIZ_PANCHANGA_H_ */
```

Listing - Panchanga.h

In the Arduino Mega, which runs on an 8 bit MCU, some of the numeric precision will be lost. The Panchanga comes close to the almanac, however is not as precise as a 16 bit or 32-bit system.

```
/*
 * Panchanga.cpp
 *
 * Created on: Apr 11, 2015
 *     Author: DevbNJ
 */

#include "arduino.h";
#include <math.h>
#include "Panchanga.h"
#include "Corr.h"

// ----- Reduce to 360 degrees
double Panchanga::fix360(double v) {
  while (v < 0.0)
    v += 360.0;
  while (v > 360.0)
    v -= 360.0;
  return v;
}

//-----------------------------------------------------------
// Nutation
//-----------------------------------------------------------
double Panchanga::nutation(double jd) {
  double t = (jd - 2415020) / 36525;
  double t2 = t * t;
```

```
  double ls = 279.6967 + 36000.7689 * t + 0.000303 * t2;
  double l = 270.4341639 + 481267.8831417 * t -
             0.0011333333 * t2;
  double ms = 358.4758333333334 + 35999.04974999958 * t
             - t2 * 1.500000059604645e-4;
  double ml = 296.1046083333757 + 477198.8491083336 * t
             + 0.0091916667090522 * t2;
  double d = 350.7374861110581 + 445267.1142166667 * t
             - t2 * 1.436111132303874e-3;
  double om = 259.1832750002543 - 1934.142008333206 * t
    + .0020777778 * t2;
  ls *= d2r;
  l *= d2r;
  ms *= d2r;
  ml *= d2r;
  d *= d2r;
  om *= d2r;
  double d2 = d * d;
  double l2 = l * l;
  double ls2 = ls * ls;
  double nut = (-17.2327 - 0.01737 * t) * sin(om);
  nut += 0.2088 * sin(2.0 * om);
  nut += 0.0675 * sin(ml);
  nut -= 0.0149 * sin(ml - d2);
  nut -= 0.0342 * sin(l2 - om);
  nut += 0.0114 * sin(l2 - ml);
  nut -= 0.2037 * sin(l2);
  nut -= 0.0261 * sin(l2 + ml);
  nut += 0.0124 * sin(ls2 - om);
  nut += 0.0214 * sin(ls2 - ms);
  nut -= 1.2729 * sin(ls2);
  nut -= 0.0497 * sin(ls2 + ms);
  nut += 0.1261 * sin(ms);
  nut = nut / 3600.0;
  return nut;
}


//----------------------------------------------------
//Ayanamsa (deg.)
//----------------------------------------------------

double Panchanga::computeAyanamsa(double jd) {

  double t = (jd - 2415020) / 36525;
  double om = 259.183275 - 1934.142008333206 * t
    + 0.0020777778 * t * t
             + 0.0000022222222 * t * t * t;

  double ls = 279.696678 + 36000.76892 * t + 0.0003025
    * t * t;
```

```
  double aya = 17.23 * sin(d2r * om) + 1.27
    * sin(d2r * ls * 2)
    - (5025.64 + 1.11 * t) * t;
  aya = (aya - 80861.27) / 3600.0;
    // 84038.27 = Fagan-Bradley, 80861.27 = Lahiri
  return aya;
}


//-----------------------------------------------------------
// Calculation Geocentric ecliptic longitude of Moon
// and angular speed.
// (accuracy 2 sec. of long.)
//-----------------------------------------------------------

double Panchanga::computeMoon(double jd) {
  Corr corrMoon[93] = {
    { 0, 0, 0, 4, 13.902 },
    { 0, 0, 0, 2, 2369.912 },
    { 1, 0, 0, 4, 1.979    },
    { 1, 0, 0, 2, 191.953 },
    { 1, 0, 0, 0, 22639.500 },
    { 1, 0, 0, -2, -4586.465 },
    { 1, 0, 0, -4, -38.428   },
    { 1, 0, 0, -6, -0.393 },
    { 0, 1, 0, 4, -0.289 },
    { 0, 1, 0, 2, -24.420 },
    { 0, 1, 0, 0, -668.146 },
    { 0, 1, 0, -2, -165.145 },
    { 0, 1, 0, -4, -1.877 },
    { 0, 0, 0, 3, 0.403 },
    { 0, 0, 0, 1, -125.154},
    { 2, 0, 0, 4, 0.213 },
    { 2, 0, 0, 2, 14.387 },
    { 2, 0, 0, 0, 769.016},
    { 2, 0, 0, -2, -211.656 },
    { 2, 0, 0, -4, -30.773},
    { 2, 0, 0, -6, -0.570 },
    { 1, 1, 0, 2, -2.921 },
    { 1, 1, 0, 0, -109.673 },
    { 1, 1, 0, -2, -205.962},
    { 1, 1, 0, -4, -4.391 },
    { 1, -1, 0, 4, 0.283 },
    { 1, -1, 0, 2, 14.577 },
    { 1, -1, 0, 0, 147.687 },
    { 1, -1, 0, -2, 28.475},
    { 1, -1, 0, -4, 0.636 },
    { 0, 2, 0, 2, -0.189 },
    { 0, 2, 0, 0, -7.486},
    { 0, 2, 0, -2, -8.096 },
    { 0, 0, 2, 2, -5.741},
    { 0, 0, 2, 0, -411.608 },
    { 0, 0, 2, -2, -55.173 },
```

```
{ 0, 0, 2, -4, 0.025 },
{ 1, 0, 0, 1,-8.466},
{ 1, 0, 0, -1, 18.609 },
{ 1, 0, 0, -3, 3.215 },
{ 0, 1, 0, 1, 18.023 },
{ 0, 1, 0, -1, 0.560 },
{ 3, 0, 0, 2, 1.060},
{ 3, 0, 0, 0, 36.124 },
{ 3, 0, 0, -2, -13.193 },
{ 3, 0, 0, -4, -1.187 },
{ 3, 0, 0, -6, -0.293 },
{ 2, 1, 0, 2, -0.290 },
{ 2, 1, 0, 0, -7.649 },
{ 2, 1, 0, -2, -8.627 },
{ 2, 1, 0, -4, -2.740 },
{ 2, -1, 0, 2, 1.181},
{ 2, -1, 0, 0, 9.703 },
{ 2, -1, 0, -2, -2.494 },
{ 2, -1, 0, -4, 0.360 },
{ 1, 2, 0, 0, -1.167 },
{ 1, 2, 0, -2, -7.412},
{ 1, 2, 0, -4, -0.311 },
{ 1, -2, 0, 2, 0.757 },
{ 1, -2, 0, 0, 2.580 },
{ 1, -2, 0, -2, 2.533},
{ 0, 3, 0, -2, -0.344 },
{ 1, 0, 2, 2, -0.992 },
{ 1, 0, 2, 0, -45.099},
{ 1, 0, 2, -2, -0.179 },
{ 1, 0, -2, 2, -6.382},
{ 1, 0, -2, 0, 39.528 },
{ 1, 0, -2, -2, 9.366 },
{ 0, 1, 2, 0, 0.415 },
{ 0, 1, 2, -2, -2.152},
{ 0, 1, -2, 2, -1.440 },
{ 0, 1, -2, -2, 0.384 },
{ 2, 0, 0, 1, -0.586 },
{ 2, 0, 0, -1, 1.750 },
{ 2, 0, 0, -3, 1.225 },
{ 1, 1, 0, 1, 1.267 },
{ 1, -1, 0, -1, -1.089},
{ 0, 0, 2, -1, 0.584 },
{ 4, 0, 0, 0, 1.938 },
{ 4, 0, 0, -2, -0.952},
{ 3, 1, 0, 0, -0.551 },
{ 3, 1, 0, -2, -0.482},
{ 3, -1, 0, 0, 0.681 },
{ 2, 0, 2, 0, -3.996 },
{ 2, 0, 2, -2, 0.557 },
{ 2, 0, -2, 2, -0.459},
{ 2, 0, -2, 0, -1.298 },
{ 2, 0, -2, -2, 0.538 },
```

```
  { 1,  1, -2, -2,  0.426 },
  { 1, -1,  2,  0, -0.304 },
  { 1, -1, -2,  2,-0.372},
  { 0,  0,  4,  0,  0.418 },
  { 2, -1,  0, -1, -0.352 }
};

Corr2 corrMoon2[27] = {
  { 0.127,  0,  0,  0,  6 },
  { -0.151,  0,  2,  0, -4 },
  { -0.085,  0,  0,  2,  4},
  { 0.150,  0,  1,  0,  3 },
  { -0.091,  2,  1,  0, -6 },
  { -0.103,  0,  3,  0,  0 },
  { -0.301,  1,  0,  2,-4},
  { 0.202,  1,  0, -2, -4 },
  { 0.137,  1,  1,  0, -1 },
  { 0.233,  1,  1,  0, -3 },
  { -0.122,  1, -1,  0,  1 },
  { -0.276,  1, -1,  0, -3},
  { 0.255,  0,  0,  2,  1 },
  { 0.254,  0,  0,  2, -3 },
  { -0.100,  3,  1,  0, -4 },
  { -0.183,  3, -1,  0, -2 },
  { -0.297,  2,  2,  0, -2},
  { -0.161,  2,  2,  0, -4 },
  { 0.197,  2, -2,  0,  0 },
  { 0.254,  2, -2,  0, -2 },
  { -0.250,  1,  3,  0, -2 },
  { -0.123,  2,  0,  2,  2},
  { 0.173,  2,  0, -2, -4 },
  { 0.263,  1,  1,  2,  0 },
  { 0.130,  3,  0,  0, -1},
  { 0.113,  5,  0,  0,  0 },
  { 0.092,  3,  0,  2, -2}
};

// Days from epoch 1900:
double tdays = jd - 2415020.0;
// Time in Julian centuries from epoch 1900:
double t = tdays / 36525.0;
double t2 = t * t;
double t3 = t * t * t;
// inclination of an ecliptic to equator:
double ob = 23.452294 - 0.0130125 * t - 0.00000164
  * t2 + 0.000000503 * t3;
// moon's mean longitude:
double l = 270.4337361 + 13.176396544528099
  * tdays - 5.86 * t2 / 3600
  + 0.0068 * t3 / 3600;
```

```
// elongation of moon from sun:
double d = 350.7374861110581 + 445267.1142166667
   * t - t2 * 1.436111132303874e-3
   + 0.0000018888889 * t3;
//    moon's perihel:
double pe = 334.329556 + 14648522.52
   * t / 3600 - 37.17 * t2 / 3600
   - 0.045 * t3 / 3600;
//    sun's mean anomaly:
double ms = 358.4758333333334 + 35999.04974999958
   * t - t2 * 1.500000059604645e-4 - t3
   * 3.3333333623078e-6;
//    moon's mean anomaly:
double ml = fix360(l - pe);
//    moon's mean node:
double om = 259.183275 - 6962911.23 * t / 3600
   + 7.48 * t2 / 3600 + 0.008 * t3 / 3600;
//    moon's mean longitude, counted from node:
double f = fix360(l - om);
//        The periodic corrections:
double r2rad = 360.0 * d2r;
double tb = tdays * 1e-12;
double t2c = tdays * tdays * 1e-16; // *10^16
double a1 = sin(r2rad * (0.53733431 - 10104982 * tb
   + 191 * t2c));
double a2 = sin(r2rad * (0.71995354 - 147094228
   * tb + 43 * t2c));
double c2 = cos(r2rad * (0.71995354 - 147094228
   * tb + 43 * t2c));
double a3 = sin(r2rad * (0.14222222 + 1536238 * tb));
double a4 = sin(r2rad * (0.48398132 - 147269147
   * tb + 43 * t2c));
double c4 = cos(r2rad * (0.48398132 - 147269147
   * tb + 43 * t2c));
double a5 = sin(r2rad * (0.52453688 - 147162675
   * tb + 43 * t2c));
double a6 = sin(r2rad * (0.84536324 - 11459387 * tb));
double a7 = sin(r2rad * (0.23363774 + 1232723
   * tb + 191 * t2c));
double a8 = sin(r2rad * (0.58750000 + 9050118 * tb));
double a9 = sin(r2rad * (0.61043085 - 67718733 * tb));
double dlm = 0.84 * a3 + 0.31 * a7 + 14.27 * a1
   + 7.261 * a2 + 0.282 * a4
             + 0.237 * a6;
double dpm = -2.1 * a3 - 2.076 * a2 - 0.840
   * a4 - 0.593 * a6;
double dkm = 0.63 * a3 + 95.96 * a2 + 15.58
   * a4 + 1.86 * a5;
double dls = -6.4 * a3 - 0.27 * a8 - 1.89
   * a6 + 0.20 * a9;
double dgc = (-4.318 * c2 - 0.698 * c4)
   / 3600.0 / 360.0;
```

```
dgc = (1.000002708 + 139.978 * dgc);
ml = d2r * (ml + (dlm - dpm) / 3600.0);
  // moon's mean anomaly
ms = d2r * (ms + dls / 3600.0);
  // sun's mean anomaly
f = d2r * (f + (dlm - dkm) / 3600.0);
  // moon's mean longitude, counted from node
d = d2r * (d + (dlm - dls) / 3600.0);
  // elongation of moon from sun

double lk = 0;
double lk1 = 0;
double sk = 0;
double sinp = 0;
double nib = 0;
double g1c = 0;

double i1corr = 1.0 - 6.8320e-8 * tdays;
double i2corr = dgc * dgc;
uint8_t i;
for (i = 0; i < 93; i++) {
  // indignation in a longitude
  double arg = corrMoon[i].mlcor * ml
  + corrMoon[i].mscor * ms
  + corrMoon[i].fcor * f + corrMoon[i].dcor * d;
  double sinarg = sin(arg);
  if (corrMoon[i].mscor != 0) {
    sinarg *= i1corr;
    if (corrMoon[i].mscor == 2 ||
        corrMoon[i].mscor == -2)
        sinarg *= i1corr;
  }
  if (corrMoon[i].fcor != 0)
      sinarg *= i2corr;
  lk += corrMoon[i].lcor * sinarg;
}

for (i = 0; i < 27; i++) {
  // indignation in a longitude additional
  double arg = corrMoon2[i].ml * ml
      + corrMoon2[i].ms * ms
      + corrMoon2[i].f * f + corrMoon2[i].d * d;
  double sinarg = sin(arg);
  lk1 += corrMoon2[i].l * sinarg;
}

//          Indignation from planets:
double dlid = 0.822 * sin(r2rad
      * (0.32480 - 0.0017125594 * tdays));
dlid += 0.307 * sin(r2rad
      * (0.14905 - 0.0034251187 * tdays));
```

```
dlid += 0.348 * sin(r2rad
        * (0.68266 - 0.0006873156 * tdays));
dlid += 0.662 * sin(r2rad
        * (0.65162 + 0.0365724168 * tdays));
dlid += 0.643 * sin(r2rad
        * (0.88098 - 0.0025069941 * tdays));
dlid += 1.137 * sin(r2rad
        * (0.85823 + 0.0364487270 * tdays));
dlid += 0.436 * sin(r2rad
        * (0.71892 + 0.0362179180 * tdays));
dlid += 0.327 * sin(r2rad
      * (0.97639 + 0.0001734910 * tdays));
l = l + nutation(jd) + (dlm + lk + lk1 + dlid) / 3600.0;
lMoonYoga = l;

l = fix360(l);
//        Moon's angular speed (deg/day):
double vl = 13.176397;
vl = vl + 1.434006 * cos(ml);
vl = vl + .280135 * cos(2 * d);
vl = vl + .251632 * cos(2 * d - ml);
vl = vl + .09742 * cos(2 * ml);
vl = vl - .052799 * cos(2 * f);
vl = vl + .034848 * cos(2 * d + ml);
vl = vl + .018732 * cos(2 * d - ms);
vl = vl + .010316 * cos(2 * d - ms - ml);
vl = vl + .008649 * cos(ms - ml);
vl = vl - .008642 * cos(2 * f + ml);
vl = vl - .007471 * cos(ms + ml);
vl = vl - .007387 * cos(d);
vl = vl + .006864 * cos(3 * ml);
vl = vl + .00665 * cos(4 * d - ml);
vl = vl + .003523 * cos(2 * d + 2 * ml);
vl = vl + .003377 * cos(4 * d - 2 * ml);
vl = vl + .003287 * cos(4 * d);
vl = vl - .003193 * cos(ms);
vl = vl - .003003 * cos(2 * d + ms);
vl = vl + .002577 * cos(ml - ms + 2 * d);
vl = vl - .002567 * cos(2 * f - ml);
vl = vl - .001794 * cos(2 * d - 2 * ml);
vl = vl - .001716 * cos(ml - 2 * f - 2 * d);
vl = vl - .001698 * cos(2 * d + ms - ml);
vl = vl - .001415 * cos(2 * d + 2 * f);
vl = vl + .001183 * cos(2 * ml - ms);
vl = vl + .00115 * cos(d + ms);
vl = vl - .001035 * cos(d + ml);
vl = vl - .001019 * cos(2 * f + 2 * ml);
vl = vl - .001006 * cos(ms + 2 * ml);

skar = vl;
return l;
}
```

```
//----------------------------------------------------------
//Solution of the Kepler equation (in radians)
//----------------------------------------------------------
double Panchanga::kepler(double m, double xe, double re) {
  m *= d2r;
  double u0 = m;
  re *= d2r;
  double delta = 1;
  while (abs(delta) >= re) {
    delta = (m + xe * sin(u0) - u0) / (1 - xe * cos(u0));
    u0 += delta;
  }
  return u0;
}


//----------------------------------------------------------
//Calculation Geocentric ecliptic longitude of Sun
//(accuracy 1 sec. of long.)
//----------------------------------------------------------
double Panchanga::computeSun(double jd) {
  //     Days from epoch 1900:
  double tdays = jd - 2415020;
  //     Time in Julian centuries from epoch 1900:
  double t = tdays / 36525;
  double t2 = t * t;
  double t3 = t * t * t;
  //     sun's mean longitude:
  double ls = 279.696678 + 0.9856473354 * tdays
    + 1.089 * t2 / 3600;
  //     sun's perihel:
  double pes = 101.220833 + 6189.03 * t / 3600
    + 1.63 * t2 / 3600
              + 0.012 * t3 / 3600;
  //     sun's mean anomaly:
  double ms = fix360(ls - pes + 180);
  //     longperiodic terms:
  double g = ms
            + (0.266 * sin((31.8 + 119.0 * t) * d2r)
            + 6.40 * sin((231.19 + 20.2 * t) * d2r)
            + (1.882 - 0.016 * t)
            * sin((57.24 + 150.27 * t) * d2r))
            / 3600.0;
  //     sun's mean longitude:
  double oms = 259.18 - 1934.142 * t;
  //     excentricity of earth orbit:
  double ex = 0.01675104 - 0.0000418 * t
        - 0.000000126 * t2;
  //     moon's mean longitude:
  double l = 270.4337361 + 13.176396544528099
        * tdays - 5.86 * t2 / 3600
            + 0.0068 * t3 / 3600;
```

```
//    moon's mean anomaly:
double ml = 296.1046083333757 + 477198.8491083336
        * t + 0.0091916667090522 * t2
        + 0.0000143888893 * t3;
//    mean longitude of earth:
double le = 99.696678 + 0.9856473354 * tdays
        + 1.089 * t2 / 3600;
//    moon's mean node longitude:
double om = 259.183275 - 6962911.23 * t / 3600
        + 7.48 * t2 / 3600
        + 0.008 * t3 / 3600;
//    the Kepler equation:
double u = kepler(g, ex, 0.0000003);
//    sun's true anomaly:
double b = sqrt((1 + ex) / (1 - ex));
double truanom = 0;
if (abs(pi - u) < 1.0e-10)
  truanom = u;
else
  truanom = 2.0 * atan(b * tan(u / 2.0));
truanom = fix360(truanom * r2d);
double u1 = (153.23 + 22518.7541 * t) * d2r;
double u2 = (216.57 + 45037.5082 * t) * d2r;
double u3 = (312.69 + 32964.3577 * t) * d2r;
double u4 = (350.74 + 445267.1142 * t - 0.00144 * t2)
            * d2r;
double u6 = (353.4 + 65928.71550000001 * t) * d2r;
double u5 = (315.6 + 893.3 * t) * d2r;
double dl = 0.00134 * cos(u1);
dl += 0.00154 * cos(u2);
dl += 0.002 * cos(u3);
dl += 0.00179 * sin(u4);
dl += 0.202 * sin(u5) / 3600;
double dr = 0.00000543 * sin(u1);
dr += 0.00001575 * sin(u2);
dr += 0.00001627 * sin(u3);
dr += 0.00003076 * cos(u4);
dr += 9.26999999e-06 * sin(u6);
//      sun's true longitude (deg.):
double il = ls + dl + truanom - ms;
//      aberracion (deg):
double r1 = 1.0000002 * (1 - ex * ex) /
      (1 + ex * cos(truanom * d2r));
double rs = r1 + dr; // radius-vector
double ab = (20.496 * (1 - ex * ex) / rs) / 3600.0;
ls = il + nutation(jd) - ab;
// visible longitude of sun
lSunYoga = ls;
ls = fix360(ls);
return ls;
}
```

```
//------------------------------------------------------------
//Julian day from calendar day
//------------------------------------------------------------
double Panchanga::mdy2julian(long m, long d, long y) {
  unsigned long im = (12 * y);
  im += 57600;
  im = im + m - 3;
  Serial.print("im=");
  Serial.println(im);
  double j1 = (2 * (im - floor(im / 12) * 12) + 7 + 365
    * im) / 12;
  Serial.print("j1=");
  Serial.println(j1);
  double j = (floor(j1) + d + floor(im / 48.0)) - 32083;
  if (j > 2299171.0) {
    j += floor(im / 4800.0);
    j = j - floor(im / 1200.0) + 38.0;
  }
  j -= 0.5;
  return j;
}
//------------------------------------------------------------
//Returns delta t (in julian days) from universal time (h.)
//------------------------------------------------------------
double Panchanga::dTime(double jd) {
  //    delta t from 1620 to 2010 (sec.):
  double efdt[] = { 124.0, 85.0, 62.0, 48.0, 37.0,
    26.0, 16.0, 10.0, 9.0,
    10.0, 11.0, 11.0, 12.0,
    13.0, 15.0, 16.0, 17.0,
    17.0, 13.7, 12.5,
    12.0, 7.5, 5.7, 7.1,
    7.9, 1.6, -5.4, -5.9,
    -2.7, 10.5, 21.2, 24.0,
    24.3, 29.2, 33.2, 40.2,
    50.5, 56.9, 65.7, 75.5
    };
  calData(jd);
  double dgod = kyear + (kmonth - 1) / 12.0
    + (kday - 1) / 365.25;
  double t = (jd - 2378497.0) / 36525.0;
  unsigned long i1 = 0;
  double di = 0;
  double dt = 0;
  if (dgod >= 1620 && dgod < 2010) {
    i1 = floor((dgod - 1620.0) / 10.0);
    di = dgod - (1620.0 + i1 * 10.0);
    dt = (efdt[i1] + ((efdt[i1 + 1] - efdt[i1]) * di)
        / 10.0);
  } else {
    if (dgod >= 2010)
      dt = 25.5 * t * t - 39.0;
```

```
    if (dgod >= 948 && dgod < 1620)
      dt = 25.5 * t * t;
    if (dgod < 948)
      dt = 1361.7 + 320.0 * t + 44.3 * t * t;
  }
  dt /= 3600.0;
  return dt;
}
//--------------------------------------------------------
//Calendar day from Julian Day
//--------------------------------------------------------
void Panchanga::calData(double jd) {
  char s[16] = "";
  double z1 = jd + 0.5;
  unsigned long z2 = floor(z1);
  double f = z1 - z2;
  double a = 0;
  double alf = 0;
  if (z2 < 2299161.0)
    a = z2;
  else {
    alf = floor((z2 - 1867216.25) / 36524.25);
    a = z2 + 1 + alf - floor(alf / 4);
  }
  double b = a + 1524;
  double c = floor((b - 122.1) / 365.25);
  double d = floor(365.25 * c);
  double e = floor((b - d) / 30.6001);
  double days = b - d - floor(30.6001 * e) + f;
  kday = floor(days);
  if (e < 13.5)
    kmonth = e - 1;
  else
    kmonth = e - 13;
  if (kmonth > 2.5)
    kyear = c - 4716;
  if (kmonth < 2.5)
    kyear = c - 4715;
  long hh1 = (days - kday) * 24;
  khour = floor(hh1);
  kminute = hh1 - khour;
  ksecond = kminute * 60;
  kminute = floor(ksecond);
  ksecond = floor((ksecond - kminute) * 60);
}

unsigned int Panchanga::tithi(double jd, long n1,
    double tzone, int len) {
  unsigned int s_t = 0;
  int flag;
  double lSun0 = 0.0;
  double lMoon0 = 0.0;
```

```
  double jdt = jd;
  long knv = floor((((jd - 2415020) / 365.25) * 12.3685);
  unsigned int itit;
  for (itit = n1; itit < (n1 + 2); ++itit) {
    int aspect = len * itit;
    flag = 0;
    if (aspect == 0) {
      jdt = novolun(jd, knv);
      flag = 1;
    }
    if (aspect == 360) {
      jdt = novolun(jd, (knv + 1));
      flag = 1;
    }
    while (flag < 1) {
      lSun0 = computeSun(jdt);
      lMoon0 = computeMoon(jdt);
      double a = fix360(lSun0 + aspect);
      double asp1 = a - lMoon0;
      if (asp1 > 180)
        asp1 -= 360;
      if (asp1 < -180)
        asp1 += 360;
      flag = 1;
      if (abs(asp1) > 0.001) {
        jdt += (asp1 / (skar - 1));
        flag = 0;
      }
    }
  }
  return s_t;
}

double Panchanga::novolun(double jd, long knv) {
  double t = (jd - 2415020) / 36525;
  double t2 = t * t;
  double t3 = t * t * t;
  double jdnv = 2415020.75933 + 29.53058868
    * knv + 0.0001178 * t2
    - 0.000000155 * t3;
  jdnv += 0.00033 * sin((166.56 + 132.87
      * t - 0.009173 * t2) * d2r);
  double m = 359.2242 + 29.10535608
      * knv - 0.0000333 * t2 - 0.00000347 * t3;
  double ml = 306.0253 + 385.81691806
      * knv + 0.0107306 * t2
          + 0.00001236 * t3;
  double f = 21.2964 + 390.67050646
      * knv - 0.0016528 * t2 - 0.00000239 * t3;
  m *= d2r;
  ml *= d2r;
  f *= d2r;
```

```
    double djd = (0.1734 - 0.000393 * t) * sin(m);
    djd += 0.0021 * sin(2 * m);
    djd -= 0.4068 * sin(ml);
    djd += 0.0161 * sin(2 * ml);
    djd -= 0.0004 * sin(3 * ml);
    djd += 0.0104 * sin(2 * f);
    djd -= 0.0051 * sin(m + ml);
    djd -= 0.0074 * sin(m - ml);
    djd += 0.0004 * sin(2 * f + m);
    djd -= 0.0004 * sin(2 * f - m);
    djd -= 0.0006 * sin(2 * f + ml);
    djd += 0.001 * sin(2 * f - ml);
    djd += 0.0005 * sin(m + 2 * ml);
    jdnv += djd;
    return jdnv;
}

void Panchanga::initialize_panchanga(uint8_t dd,
    uint8_t mm, int yy, uint8_t hi,
    uint8_t mi, int tz) {
  n_tithi = 1;
  n_naksh = 1;
  ayanamsa = 0.0;
  unsigned int day = dd;
  unsigned int mon = mm;
  unsigned int year = yy;
  double hr = hi;
  unsigned int inpmin = mi;
  hr += inpmin / 60.0;
  double hh = hr;
  double tzone = tz;

  double dayhr = day + hr / 24;
  long n_wday = 0;

  double jd0 = mdy2julian(mon, day, year);
  double jdut = jd0 + ((hr - tzone) / 24.0);
  double dt = dTime(jdut);
  double jd = jdut + dt / 24.0;
  ayanamsa = computeAyanamsa(jd);
  // Meant for debugging only
  Serial.print("Ayanamsa: ");
  Serial.println(ayanamsa);
  lMoon = computeMoon(jd);
  Serial.print("Moon: ");
  Serial.println(lMoon);
  lMoon1 = computeMoon(jd);
  lSun = computeSun(jd);
  Serial.print("Sun: ");
  Serial.println(lSun);
  double dmoonYoga = (lMoonYoga + ayanamsa
        - 491143.07698973856);
```

29

```cpp
    double dsunYoga = (lSunYoga + ayanamsa
        - 36976.91240579201);
    double zyoga = dmoonYoga + dsunYoga;
    double n_yoga1 = zyoga * 6 / 80;
    while (n_yoga1 < 0)
        n_yoga1 += 27;
    while (n_yoga1 > 27)
        n_yoga1 -= 27;
    double n3 = n_yoga;
    n_yoga = floor(n_yoga1);
    double lMoon0 = fix360(lMoon + ayanamsa);
    n_naksh = floor(lMoon0 * 6 / 80);
    lMoon0 = lMoon;
    double lSun0 = lSun;
    if (lMoon0 < lSun0)
        lMoon0 += 360;
    n_tithi = floor((lMoon0 - lSun0) / 12);
    lMoon0 = lMoon;
    lSun0 = lSun;
    if (lMoon0 < lSun0)
        lMoon0 += 360;
    long nk = floor((lMoon0 - lSun0) / 6);
    if (nk == 0)
        n_karana = 10;
    if (nk >= 57)
        n_karana = nk - 50;
    if (nk > 0 && nk < 57)
        n_karana = (nk - 1) - (floor((nk - 1) / 7)) * 7;
    return;
}
```

Listing - Panchanga.cpp

```cpp
#include <stdint.h>

#ifndef Corr_h
#define Corr_h

typedef struct Corr {
    uint8_t mlcor;
    int mscor;
    int fcor;
    int dcor;
    float lcor;
} Corr;
```

```
typedef struct Corr2 {
  float l;
  uint8_t ml;
  int ms;
  int f;
  int d;
} Corr2;

#endif
```
Listing Corr.h

Referring our discussions on *Panchanga*, the system is based on the longitudes of Moon and Sun. *Panchanga* in Sanskrit means five limbs. There are five means of predicting the quality of time through *Panchanga*.

First measure is the day of the week - known as *Kala*. Every day of the week from Sunday to Saturday, from Sunrise to Sunset has certain times, which are inauspicious. Hours from sunset to sunrise - roughly 12 hours are divided into eight resulting in one-and-a-half-hour interval each. *Vedic Grahas* - western planets have a lordship over each interval. Seven days have seven rulers who begin the day. The eighth interval has no lord and is therefore neither a good or a bad time. Intervals ruled by *Rahu*, *Gulika* and *Yama* are inappropriate for anything auspicious - like speaking to your manager about a potential raise, or being interviewed, plants being watered. When the quality of time improves, so do the results. This has been a Vedic practice for hundreds of years and has shown to produce results based on these principles.

Second measure is *Tithi* or phase of the moon - waxing or waning and the degrees of separation from Sun. Third is the *Nakshatra* or the twenty-seven lunar mansions, where the moon gets posited in one of these *Nakshatras*. Fourth and fifth are *Yoga* and *Karana* - geometrical points related to the *Nakshatra*.

While data is sent to the computer through the Serial Port (USB), the code below is an application in Java, which collects the data and generates and plots to a web page.

```java
/*
 * EkgReader.java
 *
 * Copyright and Product Acknowledgments:
 *      RXTX Library -
 *      http://rxtx.qbang.org/wiki/index.php/Main_Page
 *      Arduino IDE -
 * http://playground.arduino.cc/interfacing/java
 * Distributed under Open Source Apache License
 * Copyright Devb Inc. All Rights Reserved
 * Please do not remove the copyright notice
 */

import java.io.BufferedReader;
import java.io.InputStreamReader;
import java.io.OutputStream;
import java.io.File;
import java.io.FileWriter;
import java.io.IOException;

import gnu.io.CommPortIdentifier;
import gnu.io.SerialPort;
import gnu.io.SerialPortEvent;
import gnu.io.SerialPortEventListener;

import java.text.DateFormat;
import java.text.SimpleDateFormat;
import java.util.Calendar;
import java.util.Enumeration;
import java.util.Vector;

// Used by baggers
class Ekg {
    int adc;
    int timer;
}

// Used by baggers
class Hr {
    int r;
    int timer;
}

/**
 * ****************************************************
 * Main class: EkgReader
 * @author DevbNJ
 * ****************************************************
 */
public class EkgReader implements
    SerialPortEventListener {
```

```
SerialPort serialPort;
// Collect data.
public Vector<Ekg> ekgBagger = new Vector<Ekg>();
// Collect Panchanga data.
public Vector<String> panchanga = new Vector<String>();
// ADC Channel
int channel = 0;
// For all channels (in case of multiple channels)
boolean channel_do = false;
double dt1 = 0.0;
// EKG Data for the system
Ekg ekg = new Ekg();
// Buffered input
private BufferedReader brInput;
// The output stream
private OutputStream osOutput;
// Port time out in Milisecs
private static final int TIMEOUT = 2000;
// Baud rate
private static final int BAUDRATE = 57600;
// Data smoothing
int[] dataSmoothPts;

// The communication port used for EKG ADC inputs
private static final String PORT_NAMES[] = {
    "/dev/tty.usbserial-A9007UX1", // Mac OSX
        "/dev/ttyACM0", // Raspberry Pi
        "/dev/ttyUSB0", // Linux
        "COM12", // Windows
};


/**
 * method: determineCurvePts
 * @param dataPoints
 */
public void determineCurvePts(Integer[] dataPoints) {
    // Determine size
    int n = dataPoints.length - 1;

    // Compute Bezier points - right side array
    double[] rightArray = new double[n];

    // Set X coordinate values
    for (int i=1; i < n-1; i++) {
        rightArray[i] = 4 * dataPoints[i].intValue()
                    + 2
                * dataPoints[i + 1].intValue();
    }

    rightArray[0] = dataPoints[0].intValue() + 2
                * dataPoints[1].intValue();
```

```java
        rightArray[n - 1] = (8
            * dataPoints[n - 1].intValue() + dataPoints[n]
            .intValue()) / 2.0;

        // Get control points X-values
        double[] x = determineControlPts(rightArray);

        // Fill output arrays.
        dataSmoothPts = new int[n];
        for (int i = 0; i < n; ++i) {
            // First control point
            dataSmoothPts[i] = (int) x[i];
        }
    }

    /**
     * method: determineControlPts
     * @param rightArray
     * @return
     */
    private double[]
        determineControlPts(double[] rightArray) {
        int arrayLen = rightArray.length;
        // results to be returned
        double[] results = new double[arrayLen];
        // throwaway
        double[] throwAway = new double[arrayLen];

        double b = 2.0;
        results[0] = rightArray[0] / b;
        // decomposition and forward substitution.
        for (int i = 1; i < arrayLen; i++) {
            throwAway[i] = 1 / b;
            b = (i < arrayLen - 1 ? 4.0 : 3.5)
                - throwAway[i];
            results[i] = (rightArray[i] - results[i - 1])
                        / b;
        }
        // backsubstitution.
        for (int i = 1; i < arrayLen; i++) {
            results[arrayLen - i - 1]
                -= throwAway[arrayLen - i]
                * results[arrayLen - i];
        }
        return results;
    }

    /**
     * method: begin
     * @param: none
     * @return: none
```

```
*/
public void begin() {
    // System.setProperty(
        "gnu.io.rxtx.SerialPorts",
        "/dev/ttyACM0");
    System.setProperty(
        "gnu.io.rxtx.SerialPorts", "COM12");

    CommPortIdentifier portId = null;
    Enumeration portEnum =
        CommPortIdentifier.getPortIdentifiers();

    // First, Find an instance of serial port
    // as set in PORT_NAMES.
    while (portEnum.hasMoreElements()) {
        CommPortIdentifier currPortId =
            (CommPortIdentifier) portEnum
                .nextElement();
        for (String portName : PORT_NAMES) {
            if
            (currPortId.getName().equals(portName)) {
                portId = currPortId;
                break;
            }
        }
    }
    if (portId == null) {
        System.out.println("Could not find COM port.");
        return;
    }

    try {
        // open serial port,
        // and use class name for the appName.
        serialPort = (SerialPort)
                portId.open(this.getClass().getName(),
                TIMEOUT);

        // set port parameters
        serialPort.setSerialPortParams(BAUDRATE,
                SerialPort.DATABITS_8,
                SerialPort.STOPBITS_1,
                SerialPort.PARITY_NONE);

        // open the streams
        brInput = new BufferedReader(new
                InputStreamReader(
                serialPort.getInputStream()));
        osOutput = serialPort.getOutputStream();

        // add event listeners
        serialPort.addEventListener(this);
```

```
            serialPort.notifyOnDataAvailable(true);
        } catch (Exception e) {
            System.err.println(e.toString());
        }
    }


    /**
     * Shutdown Port
     * Method: close
     * @param: none
     * @return: none
     */
    public synchronized void close() {
        if (serialPort != null) {
            serialPort.removeEventListener();
            serialPort.close();
        }
    }

    /**
     * Event handlers
     * Method: serialEvent
     * @param: SerialPortEvent oEvent
     * @return: none
     * Prefix(es)
     * ADC - for analog / digital data
     * PCH - for panchanga
     * HDR - headers
     */
    public synchronized void serialEvent
        (SerialPortEvent oEvent) {
        if (oEvent.getEventType() == SerialPortEvent.CTS) {
            try {
                String xTemp = "23,09,0,21,5,2015,-4";
                byte[] vd = xTemp.getBytes();
                osOutput.write(vd);
                osOutput.flush();
            } catch (Exception e) {}

        }
        if (oEvent.getEventType() ==
            SerialPortEvent.DATA_AVAILABLE) {
            try {
                String inputLine = brInput.readLine();
                String delim = ",";
                String[] st = inputLine.split(delim);
                Integer dt = null;
                Integer tm = null;
                // For several channels
                if (channel_do) {
                    if (st[0].equals("ADC")) {
```

```
                        dt = new Integer(st[1]);
                        tm = new Integer(st[2]);
                        ekg = new Ekg();
                        ekg.adc = dt;
                        ekg.timer = tm;
                        if (channel++ == 0) {
                            dt1 = dt;
                        }
                }
                if (channel == 1) {
                    if (st[0].equals("ADC")) {
                        ekgBagger.add(ekg);
                        System.out.println(ekg.adc);
                        dt1 = 0;
                    } else if (st[0].equals("PCH")) {
                        panchanga.add(st[1]);
                    }
                }
                if (channel > 11) {
                    channel = 0;
                }
            // Only one channel
            } else {
                if (st[0].equals("ADC")) {
                    dt = new Integer(st[1]);
                    tm = new Integer(st[2]);
                    ekg = new Ekg();
                    ekg.adc = dt;
                    ekg.timer = tm;
                    // check for overshoots
                    if ((dt.intValue() > 0) &&
                        (dt.intValue() < 1025)) {
                        ekgBagger.add(ekg);
                    }
                } else if (st[0].equals("PCH")) {
                    panchanga.add(st[1]);
                }
                System.out.println(inputLine);
            }
        // On exception - do nothing
        } catch (Exception e) {
            /*e.printStackTrace();*/
        }
    }
}

/**
 * Method: main
 * @param args
 * @throws Exception
 */
public static void main(String[] args)
```

```java
throws Exception {
    // Buffer for file I/O
    StringBuffer sBuffer;
    // Initialize ekg on serial port
    EkgReader ekgreader = new EkgReader();
    // Setup the file (output)
    FileWriter fw;
    // start the ekg read
    ekgreader.begin();
    // determine start time
    long t = System.currentTimeMillis();
    // set the end time (1 minute)
    long end = t + 60000;

    // initialize the buffer
    sBuffer = new StringBuffer("var y = [");

    // wait for the thread to complete
    while (System.currentTimeMillis() < end) {
        try {
            Thread.sleep(60000);
        } catch (InterruptedException ie) { }
    }

    System.out.println("Ekg read");
    ekgreader.close();

    Ekg[] inData = ekgreader.ekgBagger.toArray(
            new Ekg[ekgreader.ekgBagger.size()]);
    /*
     * Hold this thought
     *
    ekg.determineCurvePts(inData);

    for (int i=0; i< ekg.dataSmoothPts.length; i++) {
        sBuffer.append(new
        Integer(ekg.dataSmoothPts[i]).toString());
        sBuffer.append(", ");
    }
    */
    // Heart Rate
    Hr hr = new Hr();
    Vector<Hr> vhr = new Vector<Hr>();
    int maxR = 0;
    int r = 0;
    boolean flag = false;
    int fTimer = inData[0].timer;
    int lTimer = inData[inData.length-1].timer;
    for (int i=0; i< inData.length; i++) {
        r = inData[i].adc;
        if (r > maxR) { // rising curve could be P,Q,R
            maxR = r;
```

```
                flag = false;
        }
        if (r < maxR) { // falling curve
            if (!flag) {
                hr = new Hr();
                hr.r = r;
                hr.timer = inData[i].timer;
                vhr.add(hr);
            }
            if (!flag) flag = true;
        }
        sBuffer.append("[");
        sBuffer.append(inData[i].adc);
        sBuffer.append(",");
        sBuffer.append(inData[i].timer);
        sBuffer.append("],");
    }
    sBuffer.append("[0,0]];");
    int heartRate = vhr.size() / (3 *
        (lTimer - fTimer)) * 60;
    System.out.println("Heart Rate = "+heartRate);
    try {
        DateFormat dateFormat = new
            SimpleDateFormat("yyyy/MM/dd HH:mm:ss");
        Calendar cal = Calendar.getInstance();
        fw = new FileWriter(new
            File("graph/ekg.html"));
        fw.write("<!DOCTYPE html>\n");
        fw.write("<html>\n");
        fw.write("<head>\n");
        fw.write("<title>EKG Plot</title>\n");
        fw.write("<!-- Generated code -->\n");
        fw.write("<meta http-equiv=\
                "Content-Type\"\n");
        fw.write("  content=\"text/html;
                charset=utf-8\">\n");
        fw.write("<style>\n");
        fw.write("canvas {\n");
        fw.write("    background:#000;\n");
        fw.write("    cursor:crosshair;\n");
        fw.write("}\n");
        fw.write("</style>\n");
        fw.write("</head>\n");
        fw.write("<body>\n");
        fw.write("<h1>EKG Plot -
            "+dateFormat.format(cal.getTime())
            +"</h1>\n");
        fw.write("<canvas id=\"demo\"
            width=1000
            height=400></canvas><br>\n");
        fw.write("<p>EKG Graph</p>\n");
        fw.write("<hr />\n");
```

```
fw.write("<h1>Panchanga</h1>\n");
Enumeration<String> ve =
    ekgreader.panchanga.elements();
fw.write("<ul>");
while(ve.hasMoreElements())


fw.write("<li>"+ve.nextElement()
        .toString()+"</li>\n");
fw.write("</ul>");
fw.write("<script>\n");
fw.write("var canvas =
    document.getElementById(\"demo\");\n");
fw.write("var ctx =
    canvas.getContext(\"2d\");\n");
fw.write("var w = demo.width,\n");
fw.write("    h = demo.height,\n");
fw.write("    px = 0, opx = 0, speed = 3,\n");
fw.write("    py = h * 0.8, opy = py,\n");
fw.write("    jj = 0;\n");
fw.write("    scanBarWidth = 20;\n");
fw.write("\n");
fw.write("\n");
fw.write("ctx.strokeStyle = '#00bd00';\n");
fw.write("ctx.lineWidth = 3;\n");
fw.write("\n");
fw.write(sBuffer.toString());
fw.write("\n");
fw.write("\n");
fw.write("loop();\n");
fw.write("\n");
fw.write("console.log(y[0][0]);
    console.log(y[0][1]);
    console.log(y[1][0]);\n");
fw.write("function loop() {\n");
fw.write("\n");
fw.write("    px += speed;\n");
fw.write("\n");
fw.write("    py =
    Math.floor(y[jj][0]/10);\n");
fw.write("    jj += 60;\n");
fw.write("    if (jj >= y.length-1)
        jj = 0;\n");
fw.write("\n");
fw.write("    ctx.clearRect(px,0,
        scanBarWidth, h);\n");
fw.write("    ctx.beginPath();\n");
fw.write("    ctx.moveTo(opx, opy);\n");
fw.write("    ctx.lineTo(px, py);\n");
fw.write("    ctx.stroke();\n");
fw.write("\n");
fw.write("    opx = px;\n");
```

40

```
        fw.write("      opy = py;\n");
        fw.write("\n");
        fw.write("      if (opx > w) {\n");
        fw.write("          px = opx = -speed;\n");
        fw.write("      }\n");
        fw.write("\n");
        fw.write("      requestAnimationFrame(loop);\n");
        fw.write("}\n");
        fw.write("\n");
        fw.write("</script>\n");
        fw.write("</body>\n");
        fw.write("</html>\n");

        fw.close();
    } catch (IOException ex) {
        ex.printStackTrace();
    }
    System.out.println("Done");
    }
}
```

Listing - EkgReader.java

The code snippet above is a standalone Java application that uses the RXTX library. The Library enables the application to read and write data through serial ports.

Remember to change the Serial Port settings depending on the operating system. Besides, the baud rate needs to be set in the code to the speed of transmission as declared in the sketches. The software reads the serial port upon execution and plots the data collected for a minute. It generates a web page with appropriate JavaScript to show the EKG results.

Advanced Heart Machine

The advanced system uses a 32-bit microcontroller capable of performing accurate floating-point arithmetic. Offered are several choices here starting with the Arduino Due running on SAMX MCU to TI's open source hardware MSP 432 and the TI's Wi-Fi SoC processor - CC3200.

Figure 7 - Arduino Due with Olimex EKG/EMG and OLED

It is not about *Panchanga* per-se, it is about the Moon and its phases with the Sun and positioning in Asterisms or *Nakshatras*. While these Vedic Machines run Vedic *Panchanga* or Almanac along with Kaala or quality of time while monitoring your hearts rhythmic beats to fluctuations in cosmic rays and nature, comes the need to push the readings to a full-blown computer. Reading the incoming data from a serial port on through which the MCU receives and transmit is an application software that can assimilate the data ADC and *Panchanga* and be able to either move the findings to the cloud or be able to plot the data on the computer and correlate the Panchanga readings.

The Sanskrit word *Panchanga* literally means five divisions, five principle ways of analyzing time and its quality using codes of Vedic astrology, those that relate to the Moon and Lunar phases. Unlike astrology as we know of now, the ancient - the Vedic and Celtic used Moon that is the closest celestial body around us as one that influences our mind and spirit.

Panchanga is part of *Vedic astrology* that deals with times that create material and spiritual harmony, prosperity, growth and well-being. In fact, Vedic monarchs used *Panchanga* in administrative guides and managing courts. Kings would use Panchanga to select auspicious times whose quality and energy supported their efforts.

They used the hour to negotiate treaties, enact and implement legislation, coronations, weddings, ceremonies, conception, military campaigns, diplomacy and charitable acts. With a little twist, the same principles of Panchanga can resolve problems of stress, psychiatry, health, mind and spirit and even extend to business, industry, education and personal matters. All stand to gain from the value in time that Panchanga reveals.

To determine the *Kala* or *Rahu* Kala, remember the phrase "*Mother Saw Father Wearing The Turban Suddenly*" which starts on any Monday around 7.30 AM. I found this interesting phrase at the "Tamil Brahmins" website. It takes away the drudgery of calculating every time.

According to Vedic astrology, Rahu brings about a quality of inauspiciousness. During transition of planets, the time under Rahu's influence is best avoided for any auspicious work. *Rahu Kala* is a certain segment of the day that lasts approximately one and half-hours. *Rahu Kala* is one of the eight segments of the diurnal time between sunrise and sunset. Eight segments of the day are calculated by taking the total time between sunrise and sunset at a place and then dividing this time duration by eight. Besides, *Ardhaprahar, Yamaghantak, Mrityu, Kala* and *Gulika* are five *Kala Velas* as stated in prehistoric text by Parasara.

Eighth segment is un-lorded with the first segment allotted to the weekday Lord. Other portions follow in the order of weekday Lords. We consider five portions of Grahas, ignoring that of Moon and Venus. Shares of Sun, Mars, Mercury, Jupiter and Saturn are known as Kala, Mrityu, Ardhaprahar, Yamaghantak and Gulika. For evening hours, eight parts get allotted in a different order. First slice goes to the Graha, ruling the fifth weekday Lord, counted from the day in question. Others follow in the usual order. Here again, the eighth part is Lord-less. Portions of Grahas from Kala to Gulika are the same in nomenclature in the night also. In *Phaladeepika*, *Mantreswara* in chapter twenty-five talks about the *Upagrahas*, geometrical points dependent on the weekday. Time in the Vedic system is measured through constant division of 24 horas or 60 Ghatika.

Pattern formed by Rahu Kala seems far from inauspicious as in illustration. The OM formation in the celestial sky is not a coincidence, the ancient folks were telling us something in subtle - the very poison that destroys is the elixir of life. A critic may find fallacies in the way the diagram has been shown - well, sacred geometry does not always reveal without the code.

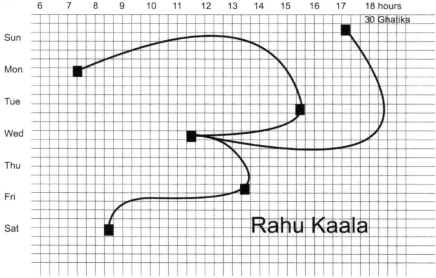

Figure 8 - Rahu Kaala and the OM formation

---

1 day = 24 hours= 60 ghatika = 3600 vighatika
1 hour= 60 minutes= 2.5 ghatika = 150 vighatika
1 minute= 60 seconds= 2.5 vighatika
1 vighatika= 24 seconds

Pratahakaala is 6 *ghatika* from sunrise or 2.4 hours from sunrise. *Sangava* is the share of 6 to 12 *ghatika* from sunrise – approximately 4.8 hours. *Madhyahna* is 12 to 18 *ghatika* from sunrise approximating 7.2 hours. *Aparahna* is 18 to 24 *ghatika* from sunrise, which is 9.6 hours, *Sayahna* is 24 to 30 *ghatika* from sunrise, about 10.4 hours.

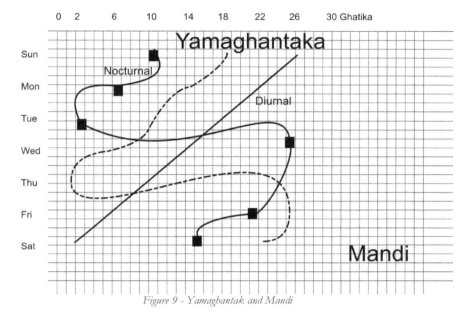

Figure 9 - Yamaghantak and Mandi

Every moment on earth is a reminder that Karma is a constant unfoldment, that destruction is imminent, birth is but a major step towards destruction; only then can one understand the Supremes' play and actions.

Reading the Ayurvedic Pulse

Nadi means pulse. From *Ayurveda* Sastra Nadi shows the three humors - *Vaata*, *Pitta* and *Kapha*. Three *Nadis* are classified as *Adi* (beginning), *Madhya* (middle) and *Anthya* Nadi (end or last part). They are also directional Dakshina, Madhyam and Uttara.

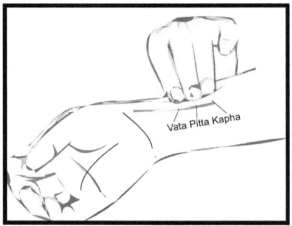

Figure 10 - Vedic Pulse Reading

To take your pulse, gently put your right arm out in front of you in a comfortable position, palm facing you, and wrap your left hand around your wrist so that your fingers fall about an inch away from the bottom of your right thumb. Ladies, your primary pulse will be on your left wrist, so do the opposite placing your right fingers below your left thumb. The goal here is to feel the pulse with little pressure. Keeping the little finger raised, the remaining three fingers should be close together and aligned - they act as your pulse sensors.

Each finger corresponds to a specific dosha - the index finger to *Vaata*, the middle finger to Pitta, and the ring finger to *Kapha*. This is the first stage of reading your own pulse. Seek where the force within the pulse is located. Which finger feels it the strongest? If properly done, this should correspond with your *Prakriti* dosha. To determine your *Vikriti*, or current state of doshic imbalance, press down a little bit on the artery with all three fingers. As you lift, notice which finger receives the initial strongest "kickback." For instance, if you feel it strongest under your middle finger, that shows a stronger Pitta presence.

Prakriti is your baseline constitution. *Vikriti* is what you have become.

For a more detailed reading of your pulse, take this a step further. True to *Ayurveda's* emphasis on nature, this technique uses animals to help commit the reading to memory. The hands are positioned the same and the fingers will still specify Vaata, Pitta, and Kapha - in that order. This time, however, you should imagine an animal you are reminded of from the movement. This might take time getting used to, but if your pulse moves in a slithering motion, like a snake or worm, it is a Vaata pulse. If it jumps like a frog or crow jumping on the ground, it is then a Pitta pulse. If it is a deep sweeping, steady pulse, like a graceful swan as it glides on the water, then it is displaying Kapha properties. A quick recap - Kapha, pitta and vaata are three constitutions in Ayurveda. Kapha designates Earth and water, heavy, cold, oily, solid, slow, stable, soft, cloudy, smooth and gross.

Meeting point of astrology and ayurveda

A striking commonality between the two methods is that astrology and ayurveda are terrestrial and bound by space and time. Taking "time" as common, applied are the two methods simultaneously to the life of an individual, community, town or nation.

The universe of the vast, the terrestrial region of earth and the inner microscopic depths are forever caught in a movement – cyclical like the seasons, rhythmic like the day and night, light and shadow; weather related – hot or cold, dry or moist. Our ability to control the microcosm to some extent and our near surroundings enables us to sway to these cosmic movements in rhythm. The more we are in tune, the better is the harmony between the two worlds. This harmony is what astrology and ayurveda try to instill through their chronicles. Ancient scriptures describe five elements that establish the building blocks for Astrology and Ayurveda. Signs, symbols and metaphors abound in the old texts, the timeless principle is the hermetic aphorism "as above as below, as within as without", and it is this statement that brings together the two methods used in pursuit of happiness. The three constitutions of kapha-pitta-vaata come from the five elemental building blocks. In Brihat Jataka as explained in Rise of the Native – Stanza 2.6 Varaha Mihira explains - Fire, earth, space, water and air are ruled by Mangala, Budha, Brihaspati, Shukra, and Sani. Surya is associated with fire and Chandra with water. In 8.22, he expounds further, different grahas give their luster of the *Maha-Bhutas* in their periods. This luster or shade has to be identified by the nose, face, eyes, skin and ear got by or through the earth, water, fire, air and space.

Space – The etheric space is empty, light, subtle – all pervading. It is stationary and formless. In the celestial world, it supports the planets, luminaries and the suns, in the microcosmic world it represents the space in the mouth, nose, tracts of the intestines and respiration, abdomen and thorax.

In the psychological sense, space defines liberation, peace, expansion in consciousness, love and expression and its opposites like isolation, separation, emptiness, insecurity, anxiety and fear. *Graha* who owns space astrologically is Brihaspati or Jupiter.

Air is dry, light, clear and mobile. As the second manifestation of consciousness, air moves in the confines of space. Air carries the electrical and ionic energy. Even though with a form, it may still be conceived by the senses. In the microcosmic world, all principles of movement as in muscles, pulsation of the heart, expansion and contraction of lungs; besides sensory and neural impulses, synaptic messages come under this category or principle. Those organs responsible for breathing, movement of the intestines and elimination of waste take part in its manifestation. At the psychological level the flow of thoughts and desires are managed within the air principle – leading to bliss, euphoria, happiness, feeling of freshness. On the extreme, it can also aggravate fear, anxiety, insecurity and nervousness. In astrological construct, Chandra has a well-rounded body, much wind and phlegm, intelligent, sweet speech and good eyes. Besides, Sani is lazy with jaundiced eyes. He has a lean, tall body, stout teeth and rough hair. He is of a windy temperament. Going into the signs, as stated by Raphael - Gemini is an aerial, hot, moist, sanguine, diurnal, common, double-bodied, humane sign; the diurnal house of Mercury having the airy triplicity, western and masculine. Libra is next, being hot and moist, sanguine, masculine, moveable, equinoctial. It is cardinal, humane, diurnal, of the airy triplicity, and western, the day house of Venus. And then we have Aquarius which is airy, hot, and a moist sign. It is diurnal, sanguine, fixed, humane, masculine, the house of Herschel and western.

Water – the next element is water – a fluid, heavy but soft, viscous, cold dense and cohesive. It bonds the molecules through its cohesiveness. Water is associated with taste, as moisture is needed by the tongue to judge taste. It exists in the organic body as plasma, cytoplasmic fluids, serum, saliva, nasal secretion, cerebrospinal fluid, urine and perspiration; required for nutrition, cleansing and maintenance. At its worse it creates thirst, edema and obesity.

Earth is hard, rough, firm, dense, slow moving and bulky, neither hot nor cold. He imbibes mechanical and physical energy. In an esoteric description, he is crystallized consciousness. While it gives strength and stamina to the body, all structural material – skin and bones, teeth, cartilage, nails, hair come from this element. Earth is associated closely with smell. At the mental level it promotes forgiveness, support, anchorage and growth. At his worse, he brings attachment, greed, depression and produces the feelings of being ungrounded.

The five elements combine and recombine to form a multitude of qualities "Guna" and their excesses "dosha". Space and air combine to form "vaata". Fire and water get together to make "pitta", and water and earth establish "kapha". Three humors govern our psychological and biological functions. Vaata-pitta-kapha are present in every cell, tissue and organ. When in balance, when in harmony with the nascent mix of the three, they create health. When out of balance, they form a disease. It is understood in Ayurveda that when you took birth, you inherited the trio in certain percentage from your parents. This is your signature, nascent dosha mix, something that should not undergo drastic changes. However, processed and artificial food, lifestyle changes, travel, work related stress are factors that make you deviate from the original balance.

Three doshas handle wide variety of individual differences; they influence what we are and what we do. They govern the biology and psychology of our body, mind and spirit. Working in precision, they create, maintain, destroy body tissues and cleanse it of wastes.

Vaata from its elemental composition is the body air principle – the energy supplied to enable movement. All kinds of movement from locomotion to cellular. **Pitta** is the principle of fire, the energy of digestion and metabolism. **Kapha** is the principle of water – lubrication and structure. The reader is cautioned that the similarity between macro and micro world is not a forced analogy, but a careful study will reflect the ecosystem.

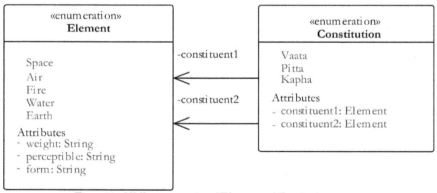

Figure 11 - UML representation of Elements and Constitution

Let me draw a symbolic view – a potter at work. Potter takes the clay which is nothing but earthen matter, which may even include waste and mixes with water and many vases, spheres, globes get fashioned. The fire makes them sturdy and dry. Soon he sets in motion the objects of his creativity, every make of his handicraft however big or small, enormous or tiny. Some may not live up to his expectations where the water or paint was more, or perhaps the baking was too strong; he destroys them to make many more. A familiar parable, but such is the cycle of life, those that fall out of synch in their humor-setup fail rapidly; those which adhere to the natural, harmonic ways survive in better circumstances. Health is about living better. The way the relationships can be represented are through various enumerations. Many enumerations leading to an architectural block. The blocks leading to an astrology-ayurvedic solution.

People with Kapha have the best physical build. They have the strongest bones, a life-long soft baby skin, may have big blue eyes, good endurance, a strong immune system and good fertility. They are people stable by nature, in their emotions and their way of thinking. People with Kapha like the responsibility, structure, care and know-how to enjoy life. From their eating habits, one can deduce that Kapha people have the slowest digestion. The folks are not big eaters; they can easily skip a meal. Without a doubt, they love sweets. When the dosha is out of balance, they eat too many sweets.

Pitta is fire and a little bit of water, light, hot, oily, liquid, sharp, mobile, soft, clear, smooth and subtle. On the physical front, Pitta people have a rather average build; they are not fat but retain good muscles. Their skin is ruddy and freckled and they usually have green eyes. They are strong people when they focus their energy and make the right choices. Pitta people like leadership and developing projects. They are very passionate in their feelings and thoughts. Pitta folks are warm-hearted and like creating things, growing and developing, indulging in beauty and luxury.

Vaata is ether and air, light, cold, dry, solid, fast, mobile, hard, clear, rough and subtle. Physically, Vaata people are built delicate, have little muscle and little body hair. They have small, lively eyes, usually grey or brown. By nature, they are not strong, they have little endurance and they are not that fertile. They are people who like variety; their emotions, way of thinking and choices are changeable. They are open and curious; they love innovation, communication and travel. Their eating habits reveal that Vaata people do not have a big appetite or a strong digestive system. By nature, they do not eat large quantities; they rather eat small portions all day long. When vaata gets out of balance, they start to neglect their diet. Many people are a combination of two doshas like pitta-kapha, vaata-pitta.

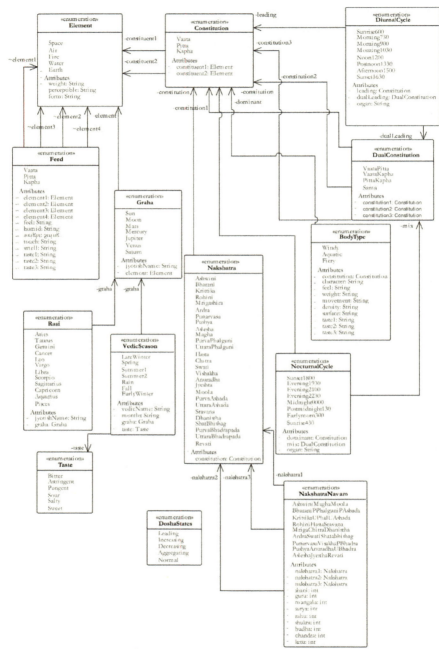

Figure 12 - UML Model for Astro-Ayurveda

52

Figure 12 styles the UML model baselined for the *Astrology Ayurvedic* construct. At the lowest level are the Elements which through combinations forms the Constitution. DualConstitution uses combinations of vaata-pitta-kapha from Constitution to generate the constructs. The BodyType uses the different constitutions. **Body constitutions** - Ayurveda defines seven types, vaata, pitta, kapha, sama and combinations thereof: vaata-kapha, vaata-pitta and pitta-kapha. The first three occur rarely in isolation and rare is the sama constitution where three doshas are balanced. On the other scale, there is the Jyotish *Graha*, *Rasi* and *Nakshatra*. **Nakshatra** classifies the constitutional types as depicted within their boundaries in terms of pure vaata, pitta, and kapha - the three doshas dealt with in *Ayurveda*. A balanced functioning of the three doshas make up the healthy and harmonious function of any system under consideration, be it on the level of psychology, physiology, sociology or ecology. The cosmos in which we live, provides a stable basis for the harmonious functioning of all its subsystems, in the sense that the three doshas are similarly distributed over the 27 nakshatras. The cyclical elements of day and night, and season is where the doshas either take prominence to being in excess or under the influence of graha. Body organs are active at certain hours of the day and night. Noting which organs are active at the time of day, night or season, and the doshas – we arrive at where the excesses are and offer the prescribed Feed.

	Nakshatra	Nadi
1	Ashwini	Vaata
2	Bharani	Pitta
3	Krittika	Kapha
4	Rohini	Kapha
5	Mrigashira	Pitta
6	Ardra	Vaata
7	Punarvasu	Vaata
8	Pushya	Pitta
9	Aslesha	Kapha
10	Magha	Kapha
11	Purva Phalguni	Pitta
12	Uttara Phalguni	Vaata
13	Hasta	Vaata
14	Chitra	Pitta
15	Swati	Kapha
16	Vishakha	Kapha
17	Anuradha	Pitta
18	Jyeshta	Vaata

19	Moola	Vaata
20	Purva Ashada	Pitta
21	Uttara Ashada	Kapha
22	Sravana	Kapha
23	Dhanistha	Pitta
24	Shat Bhishag	Vaata
25	Purva Bhadrapada	Vaata
26	Uttara Bhadrapada	Pitta
27	Revati	Kapha

Ayurveda and Vedic Healing

The ancients were adept with the Ayurveda system of health practiced in Vedic times. Vedic schools and universities taught Ayurveda among other subjects to students. Ayurveda along with Vedic astrology originates in the Vedic traditions as Vedangas.

In the Vedas, there are descriptions of methods of Vedic astrology and Ayurvedic healing. No one needs to be surprised at the relationship between the two.

The astrological signs also correspond to the doshas. Vaata is Gemini, Virgo, Libra, Capricorn and Aquarius. Virgo belongs here because Mercury rules it, which is an airy graha in Vedic astrology. It is the case also with Capricorn being ruled by the vaata planet Saturn. Pitta is Aries, Leo, Sagittarius and Scorpio. Scorpio is pitta because the classic ruler of Scorpio is the fiery graha Mars. Kapha is Taurus, Cancer, and Pisces. These are the earth and water signs not assigned to vaata and pitta. There are methods that can help decide a persons' constitution like pulse diagnosis, urine examination, facial reading and general impression.

A vaata person is slim, has difficulty concentrating, feels the cold and has a great urge to be quickly satisfied in his needs. He eats fast, chews his food badly and eats at irregular hours. A kapha is often obese, slow, and has a calm, thoughtful character. He eats a lot and enjoys his food. A pitta has a well-balanced figure, likes action and runs a fiery temper. Because his life is so busy, he may feel food is not very important.

Astrology of the three Doshas

If the ascendant is Aries a pitta sign, and the lord of the ascendant Mars is in Scorpio, a pitta sign, it will point to a pitta constitution. Grahas in the first house are also important, chiefly if they are close to the ascendant degree. Someone having Saturn in the first house is a strong indication for a vaata constitution. When a person has Jupiter in the first then that person tends to gain weight and may have a kapha constitution however, if Saturn aspects Jupiter, this tendency may be reversed.

We also need to know which planets are in the sixth house and where their lord of the sixth house is placed. If Mercury is in the sixth house and in Pisces that points to a vaata - Mercury being a vaata graha, or a kapha Pisces being a kapha sign. Jupiter is kapha but somewhat pitta graha, Sun is pitta, Mars is pitta, Saturn is vaata, Moon is kapha and Venus is kapha and somewhat vaata.

Another factor that plays a role in the analysis is the Moon's position. The Moon gives shape to "earthly" matters. Moon is an important influence on the human body. The sign where the Moon is placed - the Rasi and her conjunction with other planets can help determine the doshas. The strongest graha in the horoscope is equally important. Often this concerns a graha placed in its own sign or in exaltation and placed in a house where it can harness its own energy for example houses 1, 4, 5, 7, 9, 10 or 11. If a certain graha in the horoscope is prominent, then that planet will lend color to all the aspects of the life of the person involved, including his constitution. Every person has a unique dosha or constitutional harmony. It is mostly the dominant dosha that can become too much and ends up upsetting the harmony. When we define the dosha of a person, we have insight into a great deal of information about that person - how he functions, what types of illness he is susceptible to, what types of food he should eat and which Ayurvedic therapies are advisable. People with a certain constitution are susceptible to subsequent illnesses. At a certain time, the dominant constitution may get disturbed, become too much, and cause sickness.

Extending the Panchanga defined earlier into the context of Ayurveda. Without getting into a lot of details, a weekly diurnal clock or almanac superimposing the Doshas that rise during the day and the organs responding to the doshas and the grahas and kala involved. Let us start with day, the hour, the week and then extend to the seasons and year of how the two systems interact and the results they yield.

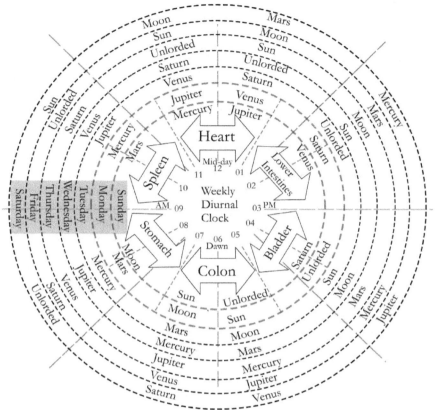

Figure 13 - Diurnal Panchanga Ayurvedic Clock

The figure is composed of concentric circles that define the seven days from Sunday to Saturday. Remember in Panchanga, the weekday start on sunrise is ruled by the graha that owns the weekday - Sunday would be Surya or sun. The day from dawn to dusk is divided into eight equal parts and the eighth part is un-lorded. You can see from Figure 11 how the rulership is distributed. Portions occupied by Saturn belongs to *Gulika Kaal*, Sun is Kala and others have their different terms as discussed before. *A Gulika Kaal* falling on the body organ Heart dominant from 11AM to 1PM calls for specific attention. I will get to remedies later in the book, but wanted to highlight the initial meeting of astrology with field of ayurveda.

Moving the lordship to the fifth, we arrive at the night duration of Panchanga along with the organs that respond to doshas at the nocturnal hours.

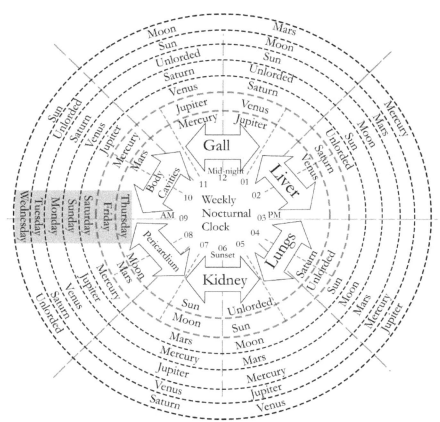

Figure 14 - Panchanga Ayurvedic Nocturnal Chart

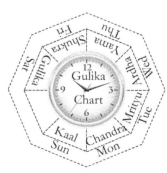

The portions of Sun up to Saturn show the periods of Gulika and similar geometrical points. Divide the any week day duration from sunrise to sunset (approximately 12 hours) into eight equal parts ~ about one and half-hours. Eighth portion is without a lord. The seven portions are distributed to the seven grahas beginning from the lord of the weekday. Portion ruled by Sani belongs to Gulika. Similarly make the night (sunset to sunrise next day) duration into eight equal parts and distribute these, beginning from the lord of the fifth by week. Here again, the eighth portion is lord-less. Sani's portion is Gulika, Surya's portion is Kaal, Mangala's portion is Mrityu, Brihaspati's portion is Yamaghantak and Budha's portion is Ardhaprahar. These durations vary in different places, as daylight may be longer in summer days in higher latitudes.

The degree, ascending at the time of start of Gulika's portion is the longitude of Gulika at a certain place. Just based on this longitude, Gulika's effects on a native can be estimated.

Way of the Native 3.65 to 3.70

From the above model, let us examine an implementation in the computer programming language of Java.

```java
public enum Element {
    Space("light","imperceptible","formless"),
    Air("light","perceptible","gas"),
    Fire("light","perceptible","formless"),
    Water("heavy","perceptible","liquid"),
    Earth("heavy","perceptible","solid");

    private String weight;
    private String perceptible;
    private String form;

    Element(String weight, String perceptible,
            String form) {
        this.weight = weight;
        this.perceptible = perceptible;
        this.form = form;
    }

    public String getWeight() {
        return weight;
    }

    public String getPerceptible() {
        return perceptible;
    }

    public String getForm() {
        return form;
    }
}
```

Listing – Element.java

```java
public enum Constitution {
    Vaata (Element.Air, Element.Space),
    Pitta (Element.Fire, Element.Water),
    Kapha (Element.Water, Element.Earth);

    private Element constituent1;
    private Element constituent2;
```

```
    Constitution(Element p1, Element p2) {
        this.constituent1 = p1;
        this.constituent2 = p2;
    }

    public Element getConstituent1() {
        return constituent1;
    }

    public Element getConstituent2() {
        return constituent2;
    }
}
```

Listing - Constitution.java

```
public enum DualConstitution {
    VaataPitta(Constitution.Vaata, Constitution.Pitta),
    VaataKapha(Constitution.Vaata, Constitution.Pitta),
    PittaKapha(Constitution.Pitta, Constitution.Kapha),
    Sama(Constitution.Vaata,
        Constitution.Pitta,
        Constitution.Kapha);

    private Constitution constitution1;
    private Constitution constitution2;
    private Constitution constitution3;

    DualConstitution(Constitution c1,
            Constitution c2) {
        this.constitution1 = c1;
        this.constitution2 = c2;
    }

    private DualConstitution(Constitution c1,
            Constitution c2,
            Constitution c3) {
        this.constitution1 = c1;
        this.constitution2 = c2;
        this.constitution3 = c3;
    }
    public Constitution getConstitution1() {
        return constitution1;
    }
    public Constitution getConstitution2() {
        return constitution2;
    }
    public Constitution getConstitution3() {
        return constitution3;
    }
}
```

Listing - DualConstitution.java

DualConstitution has two private constructors, the reason is because the first three enumerated elements have two constitution types and Sama uses three as it is the balancing constitution, though it is very rare to find a person who has the Sama type of constitution.

```java
public enum BodyType {
    Windy(Constitution.Vaata,
            "dry","cold","light",
            "mobile","varying","rough",
            "bitter","astringent","pungent"),
    Aquatic(Constitution.Kapha,
            "moist","cool","heavy",
            "structural","dense","smooth",
            "sweet","sour","salty"),
    Fiery(Constitution.Pitta,
            "hot","scorching","light",
            "changing","fluid","fetid",
            "sour","pungent","salty");

    private Constitution constitution;
    private String character;
    private String feel;
    private String weight;
    private String movement;
    private String density;
    private String surface;
    private String taste1;
    private String taste2;
    private String taste3;

    BodyType(Constitution c,
            String character,
            String feel,
            String weight,
            String movement,
            String density,
            String surface,
            String taste1,
            String taste2,
            String taste3) {
        this.constitution = c;
        this.character = character;
        this.feel = feel;
        this.weight = weight;
        this.movement = movement;
        this.density = density;
        this.surface = surface;
        this.taste1 = taste1;
        this.taste2 = taste2;
```

```java
        this.taste3 = taste3;
    }

    public Constitution getConstitution() {
        return constitution;
    }

    public String getCharacter() {
        return character;
    }

    public String getFeel() {
        return feel;
    }

    public String getWeight() {
        return weight;
    }

    public String getMovement() {
        return movement;
    }

    public String getDensity() {
        return density;
    }

    public String getSurface() {
        return surface;
    }

    public String getTaste1() {
        return taste1;
    }

    public String getTaste2() {
        return taste2;
    }

    public String getTaste3() {
        return taste3;
    }
}
```

Listing - BodyType.java

```java
public enum Taste {
    Bitter (Element.Air, Element.Space),
    Astringent (Element.Air, Element.Earth),
    Pungent (Element.Fire, Element.Air),
    Sour (Element.Earth, Element.Fire),
    Salty (Element.Water, Element.Fire),
    Sweet (Element.Earth, Element.Water);

    private Element element1;
    private Element element2;

    Taste (Element e1, Element e2) {
        this.element1 = e1;
        this.element2 = e2;
    }

    public Element getElement1() {
        return element1;
    }

    public Element getElement2() {
        return element2;
    }
}
```

Listing – Taste.java

Six "tastes" defined in *Ayurveda* are Bitter, Astringent, Pungent, Sour, Salty, and Sweet. Taste in suitable extents bring about balance in our body systems. As shown in the Java enumeration, different elements in pairs impart the different tastes. Earth and Water makes the sweet taste, Earth with Fire influences the sour, Water and Fire gives salty, Fire with Air brings about Pungency or spicy taste, Air and Space gives the taste of bitterness and Air with Earth makes the astringent taste.

Sweet is found in food like rice, sugar, milk, wheat, dates and others prompting the quality of the food to be greasy, cooling and heavy. It endorses the growth of seven dhatus in the body – plasma, blood, fat, muscle, bones, marrow, nerve-tissues and fluids linked to reproduction. Sweets aggravate kapha. Sour food is found in citrus fruits, yogurt, vinegar, cheese and many others. They are attributed as liquid, light, warm and greasy. Salted foods are salt itself. It is warm, heavy and greasy. In moderation, it relieves vaata and increases pitta and kapha, while too much salt aggravates them. Pungent taste comes from hot peppers, onion, radish, garlic, mustard and ginger. It is light, drying and warm.

It aggravates vaata. Bitter is found in coffee, chocolate, aloe-vera, fenugreek, turmeric, dandelion and sandalwood. It is cool, light and dry. It increases vaata and decreases pitta and kapha. Astringent taste is found in unripe bananas, chickpeas, green beans, split peas, Arjuna and alum. It is cooling, drying and heavy. In moderation, it reduces pitta and kapha, aggravating vaata.

```java
public enum DoshaStates {
    Leading, Increasing, Decreasing, Aggregating, Normal;
}
```
Listing – DoshaStates.java

```java
public enum DiurnalCycle {
    Sunrise600 (0, Constitution.Vaata, "Colon"),
    Morning730 (1, DualConstitution.VaataKapha,
                "Stomach"),
    Morning900 (2, Constitution.Kapha,"Spleen"),
    Morning1030 (3,
                DualConstitution.PittaKapha,
                "Spleen/Heart"),
    Noon1200 (4, Constitution.Pitta, "Heart"),
    Postnoon1330 (5, DualConstitution.PittaKapha,
                "Small Intestine"),
    Afternoon1500 (6, Constitution.Kapha, "Bladder"),
    Sunset1630 (7, Constitution.Vaata,"Kidney");

    private int id;
    private Constitution leading;
    private DualConstitution dualLeading;
    private String organ;

    DiurnalCycle (int id,
            Constitution c, String o) {
        this.id = id;
        this.leading = c;
        this.organ = o;
    }

    DiurnalCycle (int id,
            DualConstitution d, String o) {
        this.id = id;
        this.dualLeading = d;
        this.organ = o;
    }

    public int getId() {
        return id;
    }
```

```
    public Constitution getLeading() {
        return leading;
    }

    public DualConstitution getDualLeading() {
        return dualLeading;
    }

    public String getOrgan() {
        return organ;
    }
}
```

Listing – DiurnalCycle.java

A similar construct in DiurnalCycle is the variation from strict constitutional types to dual ones – leading to two private constructors to handle the enumeration.

```
public enum NocturnalCycle {
    Sunset1800 (Constitution.Vaata, "Kidney"),
    Evening1930 (DualConstitution.VaataKapha,
            "Pericardium"),
    Evening2100 (Constitution.Kapha,
            "Body cavities"),
    Evening2230 (DualConstitution.PittaKapha,"Gall"),
    Midnight0000 (Constitution.Pitta, "Gall"),
    Postmidnight130 (DualConstitution.PittaKapha,
            "Liver"),
    Earlymorn300 (Constitution.Kapha,
            "Liver/Lungs"),
    Sunrise430 (Constitution.Vaata,"Lungs");

    public Constitution getDominant() {
        return dominant;
    }

    public DualConstitution getMix() {
        return mix;
    }

    public String getOrgan() {
        return organ;
    }

    private Constitution dominant;
    private DualConstitution mix;
    private String organ;
```

```
NocturnalCycle (Constitution c, String o) {
    this.dominant = c;
    this.organ = o;
}

NocturnalCycle (DualConstitution d,
        String o) {
    this.mix = d;
    this.organ = o;
}
}
```

Listing – NocturnalCycle.java

Now to define the astrological enumerations needed to bring the two methods of ayurveda and astrology together.

```
public enum Graha {
    Sun ("Surya", Element.Fire),
    Moon ("Chandra", Element.Water),
    Mars ("Mangala", Element.Fire),
    Mercury ("Budha", Element.Earth),
    Jupiter ("Brihaspati", Element.Space),
    Venus ("Shukra", Element.Water),
    Saturn ("Sani", Element.Air);

    private String jyotishName;
    private Element element;

    Graha (String j, Element e) {
        this.jyotishName = j;
        this.element = e;
    }

    public String getJyotishName() {
        return jyotishName;
    }

    public Element getElement() {
        return element;
    }
}
```

Listing – Graha.java

```java
public enum Rasi {
    Aries ("Mesha", Graha.Mars),
    Taurus ("Vrisabha", Graha.Venus),
    Gemini ("Mithuna", Graha.Mercury),
    Cancer ("Karkata", Graha.Moon),
    Leo ("Simha", Graha.Sun),
    Virgo ("Kanya", Graha.Mercury),
    Libra ("Tula", Graha.Venus),
    Scorpio ("Vrischika", Graha.Mars),
    Sagittarius ("Dhanu", Graha.Jupiter),
    Capricorn ("Makar", Graha.Saturn),
    Aquarius ("Kumbha", Graha.Saturn),
    Pisces ("Meena", Graha.Jupiter);

    private String jyotishName;
    private Graha graha;

    Rasi (String j, Graha g) {
        this.jyotishName = j;
        this.graha = g;
    }

    public String getJyotishName() {
        return jyotishName;
    }

    public void setJyotishName(String jyotishName) {
        this.jyotishName = jyotishName;
    }

    public Graha getGraha() {
        return graha;
    }

    public void setGraha(Graha graha) {
        this.graha = graha;
    }
}
```

Listing – Rasi.java

```java
public enum Nakshatra {
    Ashwini      (Constitution.Vaata),
    Bharani      (Constitution.Pitta),
    Krittika     (Constitution.Kapha),
    Rohini       (Constitution.Kapha),
    Mrigashira   (Constitution.Pitta),
    Ardra        (Constitution.Vaata),
    Punarvasu    (Constitution.Vaata),
    Pushya       (Constitution.Pitta),
    Aslesha      (Constitution.Kapha),
    Magha        (Constitution.Kapha),
    PurvaPhalguni    (Constitution.Pitta),
    UttaraPhalguni   (Constitution.Vaata),
    Hasta        (Constitution.Vaata),
    Chitra       (Constitution.Pitta),
    Swati        (Constitution.Kapha),
    Vishakha     (Constitution.Kapha),
    Anuradha     (Constitution.Pitta),
    Jyeshta      (Constitution.Vaata),
    Moola        (Constitution.Vaata),
    PurvaAshada      (Constitution.Pitta),
    UttaraAshada     (Constitution.Kapha),
    Sravana      (Constitution.Kapha),
    Dhanistha    (Constitution.Pitta),
    ShatBhishag (Constitution.Vaata),
    PurvaBhadrapada      (Constitution.Vaata),
    UttaraBhadrapada     (Constitution.Pitta),
    Revati       (Constitution.Kapha);

    private Constitution constitution;

    Nakshatra (Constitution c) {
        this.constitution = c;
    }

    public Constitution getConstitution() {
        return constitution;
    }
}
```

Listing – Nakshatra.java

```java
public enum VedicSeason {
    LateWinter ("Sisir", "Jan/Mar",
            Graha.Saturn, Taste.Bitter),
    Spring ("Vasanta", "Mar/May",
            Graha.Venus, Taste.Astringent),
    Summer1 ("Greesham", "May/Jun",
            Graha.Mars, Taste.Pungent),
    Summer2 ("Greesham", "Jun/Jul",
            Graha.Sun, Taste.Pungent),
    Rain ("Varsha", "Jul/Sep",
            Graha.Moon, Taste.Sour),
    Fall ("Sarad", "Sep/Nov",
            Graha.Mercury, Taste.Salty),
    EarlyWinter ("Hemanta", "Nov/Jan",
            Graha.Jupiter, Taste.Sweet);

    private String vedicName;
    private String months;
    private Graha graha;
    private Taste taste;
    VedicSeason (String vname,   String months,
            Graha g, Taste t) {
        this.vedicName = vname;
        this.months = months;
        this.graha = g;
        this.taste = t;
    }

    public String getVedicName() {
        return vedicName;
    }

    public String getMonths() {
        return months;
    }

    public Graha getGraha() {
        return graha;
    }

    public Taste getTaste() {
        return taste;
    }
}
```

Listing – VedicSeason.java

I have modified and shrunk the Sunrise and Sunset Java library of Mike Reedell of LuckyCatLabs, where is Copyrighted to author Mike Reedell, released to the open source community under Apache License Version 2.0.

```java
/*
 * Original code by Mike Reedell
 * URL: https://github.com/mikereedell/
 * sunrisesunsetlib-java
 * Adapted for this book
 */
import java.math.BigDecimal;

public class Zenith {
    public static final Zenith ASTRONOMICAL =
            new Zenith(108);

    public static final Zenith NAUTICAL =
            new Zenith(102);

    public static final Zenith CIVIL =
            new Zenith(96);

    public static final Zenith OFFICIAL =
            new Zenith(90.8333);

    private final BigDecimal degrees;

    public Zenith(double degrees) {
        this.degrees =
                BigDecimal.valueOf(degrees);
    }

    public BigDecimal degrees() {
        return degrees;
    }

}
```

Listing – Zenith.java

```
/*
 * Original code by Mike Reedell
 * URL: https://github.com/mikereedell/
 * sunrisesunsetlib-java
 * Adapted for this book
 */

import java.math.BigDecimal;
import java.math.MathContext;
import java.math.RoundingMode;
import java.util.Calendar;
import java.util.TimeZone;

public class SolarEventCalculator {
    final private Location location;
    final private TimeZone timeZone;

    public SolarEventCalculator(Location location,
            String timeZoneIdentifier) {
        this.location = location;
        this.timeZone =
            TimeZone.getTimeZone(
                    timeZoneIdentifier);
    }

    public SolarEventCalculator(Location location,
            TimeZone timeZone) {
        this.location = location;
        this.timeZone = timeZone;
    }

    public String computeSunriseTime(
            Zenith solarZenith, Calendar date) {
        return getLocalTimeAsString(
                computeSolarEventTime(
                        solarZenith, date, true));
    }

    public double computeSunrise(
            Zenith solarZenith, Calendar date) {
        return getLocalTimeAsDouble(
                computeSolarEventTime(
                        solarZenith, date, true));
    }

    public String computeSunsetTime(
            Zenith solarZenith, Calendar date) {
        return getLocalTimeAsString(
                computeSolarEventTime(
                        solarZenith, date, false));
```

```
}

public double computeSunset(
        Zenith solarZenith, Calendar date) {
    return getLocalTimeAsDouble(
            computeSolarEventTime(
                    solarZenith, date, false));
}
private BigDecimal computeSolarEventTime(
        Zenith solarZenith,
        Calendar date,
        boolean isSunrise) {
    date.setTimeZone(this.timeZone);
    BigDecimal longitudeHour =
            getLongitudeHour(date, isSunrise);

    BigDecimal meanAnomaly =
            getMeanAnomaly(longitudeHour);
    BigDecimal sunTrueLong =
            getSunTrueLongitude(meanAnomaly);
    BigDecimal cosineSunLocalHour =
            getCosineSunLocalHour(
                    sunTrueLong, solarZenith);
    if ((cosineSunLocalHour.doubleValue() < -1.0)
        || (cosineSunLocalHour.doubleValue() > 1.0)) {
        return null;
    }

    BigDecimal sunLocalHour =
            getSunLocalHour(
                cosineSunLocalHour, isSunrise);
    BigDecimal localMeanTime =
            getLocalMeanTime(
                sunTrueLong,
                longitudeHour, sunLocalHour);
    BigDecimal localTime =
            getLocalTime(localMeanTime, date);
    return localTime;
}

private BigDecimal getBaseLongitudeHour() {
    return divideBy(
        location.getLongitude(),
        BigDecimal.valueOf(15));
}

private BigDecimal getLongitudeHour(
        Calendar date, Boolean isSunrise) {
    int offset = 18;
    if (isSunrise) {
        offset = 6;
    }
```

```
        BigDecimal dividend =
            BigDecimal.valueOf(offset).
            subtract(getBaseLongitudeHour());
        BigDecimal addend = divideBy(
            dividend, BigDecimal.valueOf(24));
        BigDecimal longHour =
            getDayOfYear(date).add(addend);
        return setScale(longHour);
    }

    private BigDecimal getMeanAnomaly(
            BigDecimal longitudeHour) {
        BigDecimal meanAnomaly =
                multiplyBy(new BigDecimal("0.9856"),
                        longitudeHour).subtract(
                        new BigDecimal("3.289"));
        return setScale(meanAnomaly);
    }

    private BigDecimal getSunTrueLongitude(
            BigDecimal meanAnomaly) {
        BigDecimal sinMeanAnomaly =
                new BigDecimal(
                    Math.sin(convertDegreesToRadians(
                        meanAnomaly).doubleValue()));
        BigDecimal sinDoubleMeanAnomaly =
                new BigDecimal(Math.sin(
                    multiplyBy(convertDegreesToRadians(
                    meanAnomaly), BigDecimal.valueOf(2))
                    .doubleValue()));

        BigDecimal firstPart = meanAnomaly.add(
                multiplyBy(sinMeanAnomaly,
                    new BigDecimal("1.916")));
        BigDecimal secondPart = multiplyBy(
                sinDoubleMeanAnomaly,
                new BigDecimal("0.020")).add(
                    new BigDecimal("282.634"));
        BigDecimal trueLongitude =
                firstPart.add(secondPart);

        if (trueLongitude.doubleValue() > 360) {
            trueLongitude = trueLongitude.subtract(
                BigDecimal.valueOf(360));
        }
        return setScale(trueLongitude);
    }

    private BigDecimal getRightAscension(
            BigDecimal sunTrueLong) {
        BigDecimal tanL =
                new BigDecimal(
```

```
            Math.tan(convertDegreesToRadians(
                sunTrueLong).doubleValue()));

    BigDecimal innerParens =
            multiplyBy(convertRadiansToDegrees(tanL),
                new BigDecimal("0.91764"));
    BigDecimal rightAscension =
            new BigDecimal(Math.atan(
                convertDegreesToRadians(
                    innerParens).doubleValue()));
    rightAscension = setScale(
            convertRadiansToDegrees(rightAscension));

    if (rightAscension.doubleValue() < 0) {
        rightAscension =
            rightAscension.add(
                BigDecimal.valueOf(360));
    } else if (rightAscension.doubleValue() > 360) {
        rightAscension =
                rightAscension.subtract(
                    BigDecimal.valueOf(360));
    }

    BigDecimal ninety = BigDecimal.valueOf(90);
    BigDecimal longitudeQuadrant =
            sunTrueLong.divide(ninety,
                0, RoundingMode.FLOOR);
    longitudeQuadrant =
            longitudeQuadrant.multiply(ninety);

    BigDecimal rightAscensionQuadrant =
            rightAscension.divide(ninety,
                0, RoundingMode.FLOOR);
    rightAscensionQuadrant =
            rightAscensionQuadrant.multiply(
                ninety);

    BigDecimal augend =
            longitudeQuadrant.subtract(
                rightAscensionQuadrant);
    return divideBy(
            rightAscension.add(augend),
            BigDecimal.valueOf(15));
}

private BigDecimal
    getCosineSunLocalHour(
            BigDecimal sunTrueLong,
            Zenith zenith) {
    BigDecimal sinSunDeclination =
            getSinOfSunDeclination(sunTrueLong);
    BigDecimal cosineSunDeclination =
```

```
                getCosineOfSunDeclination(
                    sinSunDeclination);

        BigDecimal zenithInRads =
                convertDegreesToRadians(
                        zenith.degrees());
        BigDecimal cosineZenith =
                BigDecimal.valueOf(
                        Math.cos(zenithInRads
                            .doubleValue()));
        BigDecimal sinLatitude =
                BigDecimal.valueOf(
                        Math.sin(convertDegreesToRadians(
                        location.getLatitude())
                        .doubleValue()));
        BigDecimal cosLatitude =
                BigDecimal.valueOf(
                        Math.cos(convertDegreesToRadians(
                        location.getLatitude())
                        .doubleValue()));

        BigDecimal sinDeclinationTimesSinLat =
                sinSunDeclination.multiply(
                        sinLatitude);
        BigDecimal dividend =
                cosineZenith.subtract(
                        sinDeclinationTimesSinLat);
        BigDecimal divisor =
                cosineSunDeclination.multiply(
                        cosLatitude);

        return setScale(divideBy(
                dividend, divisor));
    }

    private BigDecimal
        getSinOfSunDeclination(BigDecimal
                sunTrueLong) {
        BigDecimal sinTrueLongitude =
                BigDecimal.valueOf(
                Math.sin(convertDegreesToRadians(
                        sunTrueLong).doubleValue()));
        BigDecimal sinOfDeclination =
                sinTrueLongitude.multiply(
                        new BigDecimal("0.39782"));
        return setScale(sinOfDeclination);
    }

    private BigDecimal
        getCosineOfSunDeclination(
                BigDecimal sinSunDeclination) {
        BigDecimal arcSinOfSinDeclination =
```

74

```
                BigDecimal.valueOf(
                        Math.asin(sinSunDeclination
                                .doubleValue()));
        BigDecimal cosDeclination =
                BigDecimal.valueOf(
                        Math.cos(arcSinOfSinDeclination
                                .doubleValue()));
        return setScale(cosDeclination);
}

private BigDecimal
    getSunLocalHour(BigDecimal cosineSunLocalHour,
            Boolean isSunrise) {
        BigDecimal arcCosineOfCosineHourAngle =
                getArcCosineFor(cosineSunLocalHour);
        BigDecimal localHour =
                convertRadiansToDegrees(
                    arcCosineOfCosineHourAngle);
        if (isSunrise) {
            localHour =
                BigDecimal.valueOf(360)
                .subtract(localHour);
        }
        return divideBy(localHour,
                BigDecimal.valueOf(15));
}

private BigDecimal
    getLocalMeanTime(BigDecimal sunTrueLong,
            BigDecimal longitudeHour,
            BigDecimal sunLocalHour) {
        BigDecimal rightAscension =
                this.getRightAscension(sunTrueLong);
        BigDecimal innerParens =
                longitudeHour.multiply(
                new BigDecimal("0.06571"));
        BigDecimal localMeanTime =
                sunLocalHour.add(
                    rightAscension)
                    .subtract(innerParens);
        localMeanTime =
                localMeanTime.subtract(
                new BigDecimal("6.622"));

        if (localMeanTime.doubleValue() < 0) {
            localMeanTime =
                localMeanTime.add(
                BigDecimal.valueOf(24));
        } else
        if (localMeanTime.doubleValue() > 24) {
            localMeanTime =
                localMeanTime
```

```
                    .subtract(BigDecimal.valueOf(24));
    }
    return setScale(localMeanTime);
}
private BigDecimal
    getLocalTime(
            BigDecimal localMeanTime,
            Calendar date) {
    BigDecimal utcTime =
            localMeanTime.subtract(
                getBaseLongitudeHour());
    BigDecimal utcOffSet =
            getUTCOffSet(date);
    BigDecimal utcOffSetTime =
            utcTime.add(utcOffSet);
    return adjustForDST(
            utcOffSetTime, date);
}


private BigDecimal adjustForDST(
        BigDecimal localMeanTime,
        Calendar date) {
    BigDecimal localTime =
            localMeanTime;
    if (timeZone
        .inDaylightTime(date.getTime())) {
        localTime =
            localTime.add(BigDecimal.ONE);
    }
    if (localTime
        .doubleValue() > 24.0) {
        localTime =
            localTime.subtract(
                BigDecimal.valueOf(24));
    }
    return localTime;
}


private String
    getLocalTimeAsString(
            BigDecimal localTimeParam) {
    if (localTimeParam == null) {
        return "99:99";
    }

    BigDecimal localTime =
            localTimeParam;
    if (localTime
        .compareTo(BigDecimal.ZERO) == -1) {
        localTime =
            localTime.add(
                BigDecimal.valueOf(24.0D));
```

```
    }
    String[] timeComponents =
            localTime.toPlainString()
            .split("\\.");
    int hour = Integer
            .parseInt(timeComponents[0]);

    BigDecimal minutes =
            new BigDecimal("0."
                    + timeComponents[1]);
    minutes = minutes.multiply(
            BigDecimal.valueOf(60))
            .setScale(0, RoundingMode.HALF_EVEN);
    if (minutes.intValue() == 60) {
        minutes = BigDecimal.ZERO;
        hour += 1;
    }
    if (hour == 24) {
        hour = 0;
    }

    String minuteString =
            minutes.intValue() < 10 ?
            "0" + minutes.toPlainString()
            : minutes.toPlainString();
    String hourString = (hour < 10) ?
            "0" + String.valueOf(hour)
            : String.valueOf(hour);
    return hourString + ":" + minuteString;
}

private double getLocalTimeAsDouble(
        BigDecimal localTimeParam) {
    if (localTimeParam == null) {
        return 99.99;
    }

    BigDecimal localTime =
            localTimeParam;
    if (localTime
        .compareTo(BigDecimal.ZERO) == -1) {
        localTime =
            localTime.add(
                BigDecimal.valueOf(24.0D));
    }
    String[] timeComponents =
            localTime.toPlainString()
            .split("\\.");
    int hour = Integer
            .parseInt(timeComponents[0]);

    BigDecimal minutes =
```

```java
                new BigDecimal("0."
                        + timeComponents[1]);
        return (double)hour
                + minutes.doubleValue();
    }


    private BigDecimal
        getDayOfYear(Calendar date) {
        return new
            BigDecimal(date.get(Calendar.DAY_OF_YEAR));
    }


    private BigDecimal
        getUTCOffSet(Calendar date) {
        BigDecimal offSetInMillis =
                new BigDecimal(
                    date.get(Calendar.ZONE_OFFSET));
        BigDecimal offSet =
                offSetInMillis.divide(
                    new BigDecimal(3600000),
                    new MathContext(2));
        return offSet;
    }


    private BigDecimal
        getArcCosineFor(
                BigDecimal radians) {
        BigDecimal arcCosine =
                BigDecimal.valueOf(
                    Math.acos(radians.doubleValue()));
        return setScale(arcCosine);
    }


    private BigDecimal
        convertRadiansToDegrees(
            BigDecimal radians) {
        return multiplyBy(
                radians,
                new BigDecimal(180 / Math.PI));
    }


    private BigDecimal
        convertDegreesToRadians(
                BigDecimal degrees) {
        return multiplyBy(
                degrees,
                BigDecimal.valueOf(Math.PI / 180.0));
    }


    private BigDecimal
        multiplyBy(
                BigDecimal multiplicand,
```

```
                 BigDecimal multiplier) {
        return setScale(
                 multiplicand.multiply(multiplier));
    }

    private BigDecimal
        divideBy(BigDecimal dividend,
                 BigDecimal divisor) {
        return dividend.divide(
                 divisor, 4,
                 RoundingMode.HALF_EVEN);
    }

    private BigDecimal setScale(
             BigDecimal number) {
        return number.setScale(
                 4,
                 RoundingMode.HALF_EVEN);
    }
}
```

Listing – SolarEventCalculator.java

```java
/*
 * Original code by Mike Reedell
 * URL: https://github.com/mikereedell/
 * sunrisesunsetlib-java
 * Adapted for this book
 */
import java.util.Calendar;
import java.util.TimeZone;

public class SunriseSunsetCalculator {
    private Location location;
    private SolarEventCalculator calculator;
    public SunriseSunsetCalculator(Location location,
            String timeZoneIdentifier) {
        this.location = location;
        this.calculator = new SolarEventCalculator(
                location, timeZoneIdentifier);
    }


    public SunriseSunsetCalculator(Location location,
            TimeZone timeZone) {
        this.location = location;
        this.calculator = new SolarEventCalculator(
                location, timeZone);
    }
    public String
        getOfficialSunriseForDate(
                Calendar date) {
        return calculator.computeSunriseTime(
                Zenith.OFFICIAL, date);
    }

    public double
        getOfficialSunriseDouble(
                Calendar date) {
        return calculator.computeSunrise(
                Zenith.OFFICIAL, date);
    }

    public String getOfficialSunsetForDate(
            Calendar date) {
        return calculator.computeSunsetTime(
                Zenith.OFFICIAL, date);
    }

    public double getOfficialSunsetDouble(
            Calendar date) {
        return calculator.computeSunset(
                Zenith.OFFICIAL, date);
    }
```

```
    public Location getLocation() {
        return location;
    }

}
```

Listing – SunriseSunsetCalculator.java

We have set the initial grounds for our astro-ayurvedic library. Allow me to bring the two diverse systems through the common dimension of time.

```
import java.util.Calendar;
import java.util.GregorianCalendar;

import work.ayurveda.define.DiurnalCycle;
import work.jyotish.core.JConstant;
import work.jyotish.engine.Location;
import work.jyotish.engine.SunriseSunsetCalculator;

public class Panchanga {

    public static void main(String[] args) {
        Calendar tday = new GregorianCalendar
                        (2016,0,13,5,0,0);
        double periods[] = new double[8];
        int leadGraha = 0;
        switch (tday.DAY_OF_WEEK) {
            case Calendar.SUNDAY:
                leadGraha = JConstant._SUN;
                break;
            case Calendar.MONDAY:
                leadGraha = JConstant._MON;
                break;
            case Calendar.TUESDAY:
                leadGraha = JConstant._MAR;
                break;
            case Calendar.WEDNESDAY:
                leadGraha = JConstant._MER;
                break;
            case Calendar.THURSDAY:
                leadGraha = JConstant._JUP;
                break;
            case Calendar.FRIDAY:
                leadGraha = JConstant._VEN;
                break;
            case Calendar.SATURDAY:
                leadGraha = JConstant._SAT;
                break;
            default: break;
        }
```

```java
Location location = new Location("22.57", "88.36");
SunriseSunsetCalculator calculator =
        new SunriseSunsetCalculator(location,
        "GMT+5:30");
double sunrise =
        calculator
        .getOfficialSunriseDouble(tday);
double sunset = calculator
        .getOfficialSunsetDouble(tday);

double hrs = (sunset - sunrise) / 8;
periods[0] = sunrise;
for (int i = 1; i < 8; i++) {
    periods[i] = periods[0] + i * hrs;
}
int grahaNo = 0;
int cnt = 0;
for (DiurnalCycle d: DiurnalCycle.values()) {
    grahaNo = leadGraha + d.getId();
    if (grahaNo > 8) grahaNo -= 8;
    System.out.print(d.name()+", ");
    System.out.print(
            String.format("%2.2f", periods[cnt++])
            + ", ");
    String xcon = (d.getLeading() == null) ?
            d.getDualLeading().toString() :
            d.getLeading().toString();
    System.out.print(xcon+", ");
    System.out.print(d.getOrgan()+", ");
    System.out.println(JConstant.graha[grahaNo]);
}

}
}
```

Listing – Panchanga.java

What the application does is rather simple - it sets the start graha for the Kala through the day, depending on the day of the week, based on the date and other coordinates. It computes the standard time for sunrise and sunset – you could change it nautical or civil, Jyotish however uses the standard hours. Subtracting the hours and dividing by we have the eight sub sections of the day. Now each subsection is mapped to the Ayurvedic Diurnal enumeration that was defined to get the exact mapping of what the Kala is, what the organ is that is active, the doshas and their state and we will soon be working on the remedy. The results from running the above code would resemble a result as shown. Notice the hours are in decimals. To extract the minutes, you may want to get the fractional value and multiple by 0.6.

```
Sunrise600, 6.32, Vaata, Colon, Sani
Morning730, 7.68, VaataKapha, Stomach, Chandra
Morning900, 9.04, Kapha, Spleen, Rahu
Morning1030, 10.39, PittaKapha, Spleen/Heart, Surya
Noon1200, 11.75, Pitta, Heart, Budha
Postnoon1330, 13.11, PittaKapha, Small Intestine, Shukra
Afternoon1500, 14.47, Kapha, Bladder, Mangala
Sunset1630, 15.83, Vaata, Kidney, Guru
```

The human body type attributes are vaata or like the wind which is dry and cold or kapha - like water which is more structural, cool and denser and pitta – like fire – hot, light and fragrant. Vaata is nurtured by the elements fire, water and earth; pitta by elements water, air, space and earth and kapha by fire, air and space.

An example of illnesses - obesity is a kapha ailment, a red rash is a pitta ailment and rheumatism is a vaata ailment. For a vaata person susceptible to rheumatism, if he wants to avoid rheumatic complications, it is advisable that he follow an anti-vaata diet. He should eat food by which the vaata dwindles. If you recall, in Ayurveda, there are six different tastes: sweet, sour, salt, pungent, bitter and acid. Everything we eat or drink comes under one of these six tastes. The vaata person gets encouraged by overpowering, bitter and acidic food. Weakened is the dosha by sweet, sour and salt; evidently, a vaata person should eat food that is sweet, sour or salty. Everything that fuels vaata weakens kapha and so is the reverse. Kapha is stirred by sweet, sour and salty and is weakened by pungent, bitter and acidic.

Pitta is stimulated by pungent, sour and a tad salty and weakened by sweet, bitter and acid. An example of a vaata-pitta constitution - an anti-vaata diet comprises flavors that are sweet, sour and salt. However, sour and salt will aggravate pitta. The emphasis in the diet of someone with a vaata-pitta constitution is on sweet tastes, which will kindle the kapha. Eating the sweet food will shrink the chance of illness associated with excessive vaata and pitta.

It is important for a vaata type of person to rest, not to watch too much television, and rush around doing several things simultaneously. These activities stimulate vaata. A pitta type should also take care not to do things too fast. However, a kapha type must drag himself off the couch and stay active. A pitta type should also take care not to do things too fast. When a person becomes ill, the prescribed remedies are partly directed at curing the illness itself and partly to restore the harmony in the damaged dosha.

In a nutshell, people of vaata constitution should avoid bitter, pungent and astringent in excess. Sweet, sour and salty tastes help these individuals. Pitta folks should avoid sour, salty and pungent – anything that aggravates body fire. Sweet, bitter and astringent are better for them. Kapha individuals should stay away from sweet, sour and salty – anything that increases body fluid retention. Foods that are pungent, bitter and astringent help them.

A final Java class to determine what are vaata-pitta-kapha people are made of, their likes and dislikes and what works best for them. The subject proceeds to the small device intended to monitor the heart. These devices are extremely frugal. Imagine having a throw away heart monitoring device available at every bed where the potential of a patient algorithmically shows the potential of cardiac disorder.

```java
package work.ayurveda.define;

public class BalancingAct {
    Pitta pitta;
    Vaata vaata;
    Kapha kapha;
    String vaataCure[] = {"keep warm", "stay calm",
            "dont eat raw food", "dont eat cold food",
            "dont expose to extreme cold weather",
            "eat warm food and spices",
            "maintain a regular routine"
    };
    String pittaCure[] = {"stay away from hot weather",
            "dont eat excess oil","stay away from steam",
            "limit salted food",
            "eat cooling, nonspicy food",
            "drink cool, non iced drinks",
            "excercise when it is cooler in the day"
    };

    String kaphaCure[] = {"get lot of exercise",
            "avoid heavy food", "stay active",
            "add variance to routine",
            "avoid dairy products",
            "avoid iced food and drinks",
            "avoid fat and oily food",
            "eat light, dry food"
    };

    String pittaAggravator[] = {"hot, spicy food",
            "citrus fruit", "fermented food",
            "hot, humid weather"
    };
```

```java
String vaataAggravator[] = {"dry food",
        "dry fruit", "running",
        "jogging", "jumping",
        "always in a rush", "workaholic"
    };

    String kaphaAgravator[] = {"cold, cloudy,"+
        "damp weather",
        "dairy products", "wheat and meat",
        "laziness and being sedentary"
    };

    String vaataSymptoms[] = {"anxiety", "insecurity",
        "fear", "nervousness", "restlessness",
        "confusion", "grief", "sadness"
    };

    String pittaSymptoms[] = {"anger", "envy",
        "hatred", "ambition",
        "competitiveness", "criticism",
        "judgmental", "sharp speech",
        "perfectionism",
        "control freak"
    };

    String kaphaSymptoms[] = {"greed",
        "attachment", "possesiveness",
        "boredom", "laziness",
        "lethargy"
    };

}
```

Listing - BalancingAct.java

Heart Machine

In the earlier part of the book, witnessed were many complex questions that IoT brings - like what kind of things can be connected, how will they be used and what's the technology involved? While it is still quite a wild west with the machines, there is no doubt in this new innovative era, newer standards and policies are likely to evolve as we get closer to the next few years. IoT has been around for last fifteen years, the last two years has seen rapid adoption by the masses.

Continuing with emergence of open source hardware and software - ARM processors – particularly microcontrollers
- Quick growth from M0 to M4
- Emergence of SoC
- Savings in energy
- Ability to receive inputs from diverse Analog sensors

In Software
- The return of C, Assembler, Python, Java and Maker's hybrid software like Arduino, Energia
- Large influence of Linux and hybrids

MQ Telemetry Protocol MQTT a message broker protocol for machine to machine communication is now an OASIS standard. In Eclipse conference in 2014, introduced was "Mosquito", an open source BSD licensed message broker. Lightweight publish/subscribe protocol, reliable messaging, Websockets useful in M2M communications with enormous stream processing and real-time analytics occurring at the cloud was the idea behind the concept. Besides, bridges were introduced to connect one MQTT broker to another broker.

The new world of eyes, ears and sensory – which can collect, touch, see, sense, read, write information; observe, record, transmit data; offer guidance to analytics also offer useful data in space and time like Location, GPS. These sensors can be Digital, Analog or GPIO PWM – Pulse Width Modulation – Mimic Analog behavior through Digital.

As we graduate to 32 bit and 64 bit MCUs, giving them the ability to monitor temperature, pressure, accelerometer, and a heart monitor attached to microcontroller, we first look at a standalone system comprising a 32 bit MCU.

The code below is for 32 bit MCUs. First of the examples uses the Arduino Due with the Olimex ECG/EMG sensor and a SSD 3306 OLED. *Panchanga* system it refers to is as described before.

```
/*
 * sketch: due_olimex_agniheart.ino
 *
 *  Created on: Apr 24, 2015
 *      Author: DevbNJ
 *  Copyright and Product Acknowledgments:
 *      Arduino Due: Arduico.cc
 *      Arduino Due Timer:
 *      http://forum.arduino.cc/index.php?topic=130423.0
 *      Timer (RTC): https://github.com/PaulStoffregen/Time
 *      Olimex EKG/EMG Hardware / Software:
 *      https://www.olimex.com/Products/Duino/
 *      Shields/SHIELD-EKG-EMG/
 *      LCD Driver: U8Lib -
 *      https://code.google.com/p/u8glib/
 *      Arduino Board: SainSmart Due SAM3X8E
 *      LCD Screen: DiyMall 0.96"
 *      OLED SSD3306 Screen White Display
 *      Shield: GikFun Prototype Shield for Arduino
 *  Distributed under Open Source Apache License
 *  Copyright Devb Inc. All Rights Reserved
 *  Please do not remove the copyright notice
 */

// ******************************************
// Due Hardware connections
// Res *                                    *
// 3.3 * OLED VCC                           *
// 5.0 *                                    *
// Gnd * OLED GND                           *
// Gnd *                                    *
// Vin *                                    *
//
//      *                                   *
//      *                                   *
//      *                                   *
//      *                                   *
//      *                                   *
//      *                                   *
//      *                                   *
//      *                                   *
//      *                                   *
//      *                                 * 10
//      *                                 * 11
//      ******************************************
//      ******************************************
```

```
#include "Time.h"
#include "U8glib.h"
#include "Panchanga.h"

volatile boolean l;
boolean pTime = false;
boolean pDone = false;
// ADC = Analog to Digital converter
volatile unsigned int inADC = 0;
// toggle
boolean timerInitiated = false;
// Fast I2C / TWI - LCD Screen
U8GLIB_SSD1306_128X64 screen(U8G_I2C_OPT_DEV_0 |
U8G_I2C_OPT_NO_ACK | U8G_I2C_OPT_FAST);

// Needed by Panchanga
uint8_t nDay = 6;
uint8_t nDD = 11;
uint8_t nMM = 4;
unsigned int nYY = 2015;
uint8_t nHour = 23;
uint8_t nMin = 18;
uint8_t nSec = 0;
int nTZ = -4;
char buf[2];
char sbuf[15];
Panchanga pch;
unsigned int starttime;
unsigned int activetime;

void draw(void) {
  screen.setFont(u8g_font_gdr12r);
  screen.drawStr(0, 30, "Vedic Machine");
  screen.drawHLine(2, 35, 47);
  screen.drawVLine(45, 32, 12);
  screen.setFont(u8g_font_4x6);
  screen.drawStr(1, 54, "jotiz.com/vm");
}


void startTimer(Tc *tc, uint32_t channel,
  IRQn_Type irq, uint32_t frequency) {
  pmc_set_writeprotect(false);
  pmc_enable_periph_clk((uint32_t)irq);
  TC_Configure(tc, channel, TC_CMR_WAVE |
      TC_CMR_WAVSEL_UP_RC | TC_CMR_TCCLKS_TIMER_CLOCK4);
  uint32_t rc = VARIANT_MCK / 128 / frequency;
      //128 because we selected TIMER_CLOCK4 above
  TC_SetRA(tc, channel, rc / 2); //50% high, 50% low
  TC_SetRC(tc, channel, rc);
  TC_Start(tc, channel);
  tc->TC_CHANNEL[channel].TC_IER = TC_IER_CPCS;
```

```
  tc->TC_CHANNEL[channel].TC_IDR = ~TC_IER_CPCS;
  NVIC_EnableIRQ(irq);
}

void setup() {
  screen.firstPage();
  do {
    draw();
    screen.setColorIndex(1);
  } while ( screen.nextPage() );

  starttime = millis();
  Serial.begin(57600);
  Serial.setTimeout(2000);
  Serial.println("Vedic Heart Machine");
  Serial.println(">> Please input Time :
      Example \"21,53,0,25,4,2015,-4\"");
  if (!pTime) {
    processTime();
    pTime = true;
  }
  if (!pDone) {
    doPanchanga();
    pDone = true;
  }
}

void doPanchanga() {
  Serial.print("PCH, Date ");
  Serial.print(nYY);
  Serial.print("-");
  Serial.print(nMM);
  Serial.print("-");
  Serial.print(nDD);
  Serial.print(" Hour ");
  Serial.print(nHour);
  Serial.print(":");
  Serial.print(nMin);
  Serial.print(" TimeZone ");
  Serial.println(nTZ);

  pch.initialize_panchanga(
      nDD, nMM, nYY, nHour, nMin, nTZ);

  delay(200);
  pDone = true;

  // Set the timer for EKG Reading
  // TC1 : timer counter. Can be TC0, TC1 or TC2
  // 0   : channel. Can be 0, 1 or 2
  // TC3_IRQn: irq number.
  // 250 : frequency (in Hz)
```

89

```
  // The interrupt service routine is TC3_Handler.
  startTimer(TC1, 0, TC3_IRQn, 250);
}

void processTime() {
  nHour = Serial.parseInt();
  nMin = Serial.parseInt();
  nSec = Serial.parseInt();
  nDD = Serial.parseInt();
  nMM = Serial.parseInt();
  nYY = Serial.parseInt();
  nTZ = Serial.parseInt();
  if (nYY == 0) nYY = 2015;
  if (nDD == 0) nDD = 25;
  if (nMM == 0) nMM = 4;
  if (nHour == 0) nHour = 23;
  if (nMin == 0) nMin = 36;
  if (nTZ == 0) nTZ = -4;
  setTime(nHour, nMin, 0, nDD, nMM, nYY);
}

void loop() {
  activetime = millis() - starttime;
  if (timerInitiated) {
    inADC = analogRead(0);
    Serial.print("ADC,");
    Serial.print(inADC);
    Serial.print(",");
    Serial.println(activetime);
    timerInitiated = false;
  }
}


// This function is called every 1/250 sec.
void TC3_Handler() {
  TC_GetStatus(TC1, 0);
  timerInitiated = true;
}
```

Listing - due_olimex_agniheart.ino

Next we move to a similar device using the Texas Instruments open source hardware - the MSP 432 Launchpad. The MSP 432 uses the AD8232 Single Channel Heart Monitor ADC sensor. MCU with Wi-Fi transmits information through MQTT to cloud (hosted by IBM Cloud DeveloperWorks Quickstart). Decision engine on the cloud responds to the message by turning on gates, blink LEDs or sound the alarm – in our example, it plots the data.

```
/*
 * msp432_ad8232_ekg.ino
 *
 *   Created on: Apr 24, 2015
 *   Copyright and Product Acknowledgments:
 *       TI EXP432P410R Launchpad
 *       Sparkfun AD8232 EKG Single channel sensor
 *   Distributed under Open Source Apache License
 *   Please do not remove the copyright notice
 */

// Sparkfun AD8232 connected to
// MSP432P401R Launchpad
// *********************************
// 3.3V * *                 * * Gnd
// Lo+/2* *                 * *
// Lo-/3* *                 * *
//       * *                * *
//       * *                * *
//       * *                * *
//       * *                * *
//       * *                * *
//       *·* A0/Output      * *
// *********************************

#include "energia.h"
int starttime;
int activetime;
int previoustime = 0;
int cnt = 0;
volatile unsigned int inADC = 0;

void setup() {
  // initialize the serial communication:
  Serial.begin(9600);
  // PinDirModeSet(6, PIN_DIR_MODE_IN);
  // PinConfigSet(6, PIN_STRENGTH_2MA, PIN_TYPE_ANALOG);
  // PinTypeADC(6, PIN_MODE_6);
  pinMode(2, INPUT); // Setup for leads off detection LO +
  pinMode(3, INPUT); // Setup for leads off detection LO -
  starttime = millis();
}

void loop() {

  if ((digitalRead(2) == 1) || (digitalRead(3) == 1)) {
    // Leads not connected
    // Serial.println('!');
  } else{
    // send the value of analog input 0:
    inADC = analogRead(A0);   // PIN_06
```

```
  // inADC = map(inADC, -4096, 4096, 1024, 1024);
  Serial.print("ADC,");
  Serial.print(inADC);
  Serial.print(",");
  Serial.println(activetime);
  ++cnt;
}
//Wait for a bit to keep serial data from saturating
delay(1);
activetime = millis() - starttime;
/*
if (previoustime < (activetime - 59)) {
  Serial.print("Count = ");
  Serial.println(cnt);
  Serial.flush();
  Serial.end();
  previoustime = activetime;
  return;
}
*/
}
```

Listing - msp432_ad8232_ekg.ino

Vedic Internet of Things

Moving on to a true Internet of Things with Texas Instruments CC3200 Launchpad - the CC3200 is a SoC (System on chip) with Wi-Fi and a built in lightweight web server. It can handle TLS and SSL connections as well. Running above 80 MHZ, the 32-bit MCU delivers sufficient power to capture the Heart Readings and transmit to a web site running remotely. Using an MQ Telemetry Protocol MQTT, a message broker protocol for machine-to-machine communication, the data is sent to a broker running in the cloud. Mosquito an open source, BSD licensed message broker was introduced in Eclipse conference in 2014. It is a lightweight publish, subscribe protocol, with reliable messaging, and websockets that are useful in M2M communications. It also provides enormous stream processing and real-time analytics at the cloud with bridges to connect one MQTT broker to another broker. In our example, we have

▶ Temperature, pressure, accelerometer, heart monitor sensor attached to microcontroller
▶ MCU with Wi-Fi transmits information through MQTT to cloud (hosted by IBM Cloud DeveloperWorks Quickstart)
▶ Decision engine on the cloud responds to the message by turning on gates, blink LEDs – in our example, it plots the data

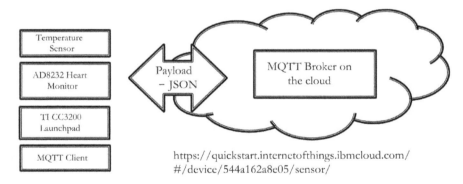

Figure 15 - CC3200 with AD8232 using MQTT

The typical lightweight payload in MQTT is in JSON format. Broker in the cloud expects to receive the device id, the label of the data and the data as comma separated values. Device therefore sends the heart readings using the mac-id as the device id and the data collected.

Separation of concerns

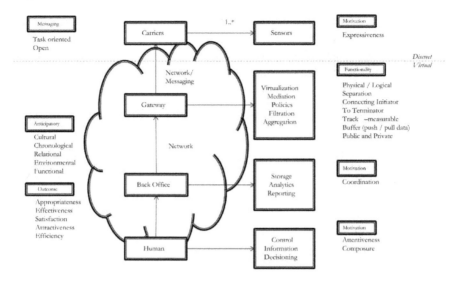

Figure 16 - Separation of concerns in an IoT Ecosystem

In the above illustration, I have shown how a typical IoT is expected to behave in an ecosystem. To the Vedic Machines, I apply a few rules which I think are pertinent to all devices that set up the things in IoT.

- Complexity may be scaled, simplicity secured. Keeping the devices simple keeps them secure. Patient information has nothing to do with heart reading and must not be transmitted with the device.
- Let the device do what it is good at - if the device has been primarily built to capture heart information, then it should be left at that. To add a complex display to it, to let it do temperature and pressure readings defeats the purpose.
- Another device should be the watchdog. A device could malfunction or the cloud could have an outage. It is not easy to monitor either, being miles away. It is advisable to set a thief to catch another. While the device is reading the heart, something else can check the battery and the connection.

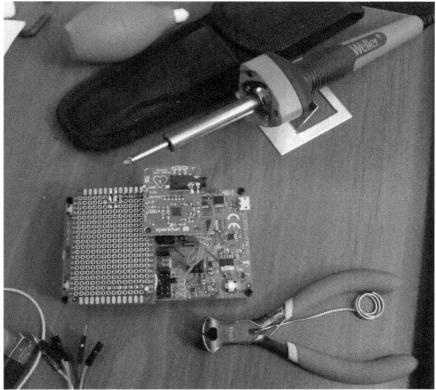

Figure 17 - The making of Heart Monitor IoT

```
/*
 * cc3200_ad8232_mqtt2.ino
 *
 *  Created on: July 14, 2015
 *  Copyright and Product Acknowledgments:
 *      TI CC3200 Launchpad
 *      Sparkfun AD8232 EKG Single channel sensor
 *  Distributed under Open Source Apache License
 *  Please do not remove the copyright notice
 */

// Sparkfun AD8232 connected to
// CC3200 Launchpad
// ********************************
// 3.3V * *                    * * Gnd
//      * *                    * *
//      * *                    * *
//      * *                    * *
```

```
//        * *                    * *
// Out/6*  *                     * *
// Lo+/7*  *                     * *
// Lo-/8*  *                     * *
//        * *                    * *
//        * *                    * *
// *********************************

#include "energia.h"
#include <SPI.h>
#include <WiFi.h>
#include <WifiIPStack.h>
#include <Countdown.h>
#include <MQTTClient.h>

int starttime;
int activetime;
int previoustime = 0;
int cnt = 0;
volatile unsigned int inADC = 0;

char ssid[] = "emryn";
char password[] = "emryn123";

// IBM IoT Foundation Cloud Settings
#define MQTT_MAX_PACKET_SIZE 100
#define IBMSERVERURLLEN   64
#define IBMIOTFSERVERSUFFIX
"messaging.internetofthings.ibmcloud.com"
char organization[] = "quickstart";
char typeId[] = "iotsample-ti-energia";
char pubtopic[] = "iot-2/evt/status/fmt/json";
// char deviceId[] = "000000000000";
char deviceId[] = "666999666999";
char clientId[64];

char mqttAddr[IBMSERVERURLLEN];
int mqttPort = 1883;

MACAddress mac;

WifiIPStack ipstack;
MQTT::Client<WifiIPStack, Countdown, MQTT_MAX_PACKET_SIZE>
client(ipstack);


void setup() {
  // initialize the serial communication:
  Serial.begin(115200);

  uint8_t macOctets[6];
  pinMode(7, INPUT); // Setup for leads off detection LO +
```

```
pinMode(8, INPUT); // Setup for leads off detection LO -

Serial.print("Attempting to connect to Network named: ");
Serial.println(ssid);
WiFi.begin(ssid, password);
while ( WiFi.status() != WL_CONNECTED) {
  // print dots while we wait to connect
  Serial.print(".");
  delay(300);
}

Serial.println("\nYou're connected to the network");
Serial.println("Waiting for an ip address");

while (WiFi.localIP() == INADDR_NONE) {
  // print dots while we wait for an ip addresss
  Serial.print(".");
  delay(300);
}

Serial.print("\nIP Address obtained: ");
Serial.println(WiFi.localIP());

mac = WiFi.macAddress(macOctets);
Serial.print("MAC Address: ");
Serial.println(mac);

// Use MAC Address as deviceId
sprintf(deviceId, "%02x%02x%02x%02x%02x%02x",
macOctets[0], macOctets[1],
macOctets[2], macOctets[3],
macOctets[4], macOctets[5]);
Serial.print("deviceId: ");
Serial.println(deviceId);

sprintf(clientId, "d:%s:%s:%s", organization,
    typeId, deviceId);
sprintf(mqttAddr, "%s.%s",
    organization, IBMIOTFSERVERSUFFIX);

Serial.println("IBM IoT Foundation
    QuickStart example, view data in cloud here");
Serial.print("--> http://quickstart.internetofthings
    .ibmcloud.com/#/device/");
Serial.println(deviceId);

starttime = millis();
}


void loop() {
```

```
int rc = -1;
if (!client.isConnected()) {
  Serial.print("Connecting to ");
  Serial.print(mqttAddr);
  Serial.print(":");
  Serial.println(mqttPort);
  Serial.print("With client id: ");
  Serial.println(clientId);

  while (rc != 0) {
    rc = ipstack.connect(mqttAddr, mqttPort);
  }

  MQTTPacket_connectData connectData =
          MQTTPacket_connectData_initializer;
  connectData.MQTTVersion = 3;
  connectData.clientID.cstring = clientId;

  rc = -1;
  while ((rc = client.connect(connectData)) != 0)
    ;
  Serial.println("Connected\n");
}

// char json[56] = "{\"d\":{\"myName\":\"TILaunchPad\",
//       \"temperature\":";
char json[56] = "{\"d\":{\"devb\":\"TILaunchPad\",
        \"heart_reading\":";

// dtostrf(getHeartReading(),5,1, &json[43]);
sprintf(&json[43], "%-4d", getHeartReading());
json[47] = '}';
json[48] = '}';
json[49] = '\0';
Serial.print("Publishing: ");
Serial.println(json);
// The MQTT protocol provides three qualities of service
// for delivering messages between clients and servers:
// "at most once", "at least once" and "exactly once".
// QoS0, At most once
// QoS1, At least once
// QoS2, Exactly once
MQTT::Message message;
message.qos = MQTT::QOS0;
message.retained = false;
message.payload = json;
message.payloadlen = strlen(json);
rc = client.publish(pubtopic, message);
if (rc != 0) {
  Serial.print("Message publish failed
  with return code : ");
  Serial.println(rc);
```

```
  }

  // Wait for one second before publishing again
  client.yield(1000);
}

unsigned int getHeartReading() {
  if((digitalRead(8) == 1)||(digitalRead(7) == 1)){
    // do nothing
  }
  else{
    // send the value of analog input 0:
    inADC = analogRead(6);   // PIN_06
    Serial.print("ADC,");
    Serial.println(inADC);
   }
  //Wait for a bit to keep serial data from saturating
  delay(1);
  activetime = millis()- starttime;
  return inADC;
}
```

Listing - cc3200_ad8232_mqtt2.ino

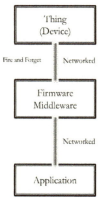

Simple Delegation. The 'Thing' can sense, it can read, it can write. The 'thinking' and 'analysis' is best done at the application. The reliability of the network, of the model is key to the delegate model. The 'thing' that is a 'do-it-all' is a misfit for this design.

Anti-Pattern. Things must be allowed to preserve their inherent nature of either collecting or acting upon another analog device. A balance of computation, data collection should be its entitlement. Conversions or curve fitting do not belong to the device.

Challenges and Successes

Storage is best managed at the application level. Storage at the device increases complexity and poses security problems.

Segregation at the unit level – it is best left for a device act a singleton. Collecting data and producing output is best left to two or more worker things. Pushing information to a device may not be feasible with many of the ULP systems which may be conserving power between intervals.

While it is all about Collect – Filter – Analyze, the challenges posed are many. I present a few which stand out as most critical.

Standard techniques used in managing things are yet to evolve. Even programming languages are still evolving and only smallest codebase like 'C' and 'Assembler' are able to address the small footprint.

Devices have different processor speeds, different timer implementations sometimes making it far from easy synchronizing these devices.

UART communication between devices and / or computer tends to be adhoc and without policies or security.

People get control through application and are informed by application. Devices are managed by the application for collection, filtration and actuating.

Substantiating through a second 'opinion' thing. If a temperature and pressure reading looks abnormal, there should be a thing to check the battery levels or a GPS to ensure the location has not changed.

Successes

Cloud is contributing factor to success of things. The things communicate through the internet. The more the cloud is involved the better the chance of success. Security is key when it comes to the cloud. The 'things' are known by their signature only. Managing the supply chain of the many parts that make the IoT is key.

REFERENCE

The code is available for download and use at
https://github.com/devbnj/agnicure

Copyrights, trademarks, product Acknowledgments:

Heart and Almanac Machine
- Arduino Due: Arduico.cc
- Arduino Due Timer:
  http://forum.arduino.cc/index.php?topic=130423.0
- Timer (RTC): https://github.com/PaulStoffregen/Time
- Olimex EKG/EMG Hardware / Software:
- https://www.olimex.com/Products/Duino/Shields/SHIELD-EKG-EMG/
- LCD Driver: U8Lib - https://code.google.com/p/u8glib/
- Arduino Board: SainSmart Due SAM3X8E
- LCD Screen: DiyMall 0.96" OLED SSD3306 Screen White Display
- Shield: GikFun Prototype Shield for Arduino
- LCD Driver: Adafruit :
  https://github.com/adafruit/Adafruit_SSD1306
- Adafruit Gfx: Adafruit - Adafruit ST3775 Shield / Sainsmart ST3775 Shield
- AD8232 Heart Monitor
- TI EXP432P410R Launchpad

Agro Machine
- Texas Instruments MSP4305969 Launchpad
- Adafruit BMP085 weather sensor
- BMP template library astuder -
  https://github.com/astuder/BMP085-template-library-Energia
- Energia Sharp Memory LCD Booster Pack -
  http://energia.nu/reference/sharp-memory-lcd-boosterpack/

ABOUT THE AUTHOR

Dev Bhattacharyya like many other authors was indoctrinated into the art of writing. In this book, the author has chosen not to let style rule over content. Dev has written books on Vedas, articles on many journals in the past and a book on technology. Dev lives with his wife and children in the northeast United States and is a prolific reader.